Histories, Meanings and Representations of the Modern Hotel

TOURISM AND CULTURAL CHANGE
Series Editors: Professor Mike Robinson, *Ironbridge International Institute for Cultural Heritage, University of Birmingham, UK* and Dr Alison Phipps, *University of Glasgow, Scotland, UK*

Understanding tourism's relationships with culture(s) and vice versa, is of ever-increasing significance in a globalising world. TCC is a series of books that critically examine the complex and ever-changing relationship between tourism and culture(s). The series focuses on the ways that places, peoples, pasts, and ways of life are increasingly shaped/transformed/created/packaged for touristic purposes. The series examines the ways tourism utilises/makes and re-makes cultural capital in its various guises (visual and performing arts, crafts, festivals, built heritage, cuisine etc.) and the multifarious political, economic, social and ethical issues that are raised as a consequence. Theoretical explorations, research-informed analyses, and detailed historical reviews from a variety of disciplinary perspectives are invited to consider such relationships.

All books in this series are externally peer-reviewed.

Full details of all the books in this series and of all our other publications can be found on http://www.channelviewpublications.com, or by writing to Channel View Publications, BLOCK, The Fairfax, Pithay Court, Bristol, BS1 3BN, UK.

TOURISM AND CULTURAL CHANGE: 52

Histories, Meanings and Representations of the Modern Hotel

Kevin J. James

CHANNEL VIEW PUBLICATIONS
Bristol • Jackson

*This book is dedicated with affection and gratitude to the
memory of two great mentors, illustrious scholars, and friends:
Alastair J. Durie and James G. Snell*

DOI https://doi.org/10.21832/JAMES6591
Library of Congress Cataloging in Publication Data
Names: James, Kevin J., author.
Title: Histories, Meanings and Representations of the Modern Hotel/Kevin J. James.
Description: Bristol, UK; Blue Ridge Summit, PA, USA: Channel View
   Publications, [2018] | Series: Tourism and Cultural Change: 52 | Includes
   bibliographical references and index.
Identifiers: LCCN 2018012561| ISBN 9781845416591 (hbk : alk. paper) | ISBN
   9781845416614 (epub) | ISBN 9781845416621 (kindle)
Subjects: LCSH: Hotels—History. | Hotels—Social aspects. | Hospitality
   industry—History. | Hospitality industry—Social aspects.
Classification: LCC TX908 .J358 2018 | DDC 647.9409—dc23 LC record available
   at https://lccn.loc.gov/2018012561

British Library Cataloguing in Publication Data
A catalogue entry for this book is available from the British Library.

ISBN-13: 978-1-84541-659-1 (hbk)
ISBN-13: 978-1-83646-035-0 (pbk)

Channel View Publications
UK: BLOCK, The Fairfax, Pithay Court, Bristol, BS1 3BN, UK.
USA: NBN, Jackson, TN, USA.
Authorised Representative: Easy Access System Europe – Mustamäe tee 50, 10621
Tallinn, Estonia gpsr.requests@easproject.com.

Website: www.channelviewpublications.com
Bluesky: https://bsky.app/profile/multi-ling-mat.bsky.social
Twitter: Channel_View
Facebook: https://www.facebook.com/channelviewpublications
Blog: www.channelviewpublications.wordpress.com

Typeset by Nova Techset Private Limited, Bengaluru and Chennai, India.

Contents

List of Figures

Acknowledgements

This project germinated within lively graduate classes, engaging scholarly exchanges and informal discussions with many students, colleagues and friends. Students in my graduate classes 'Topics in Cultural History' and its successor, 'Tourism and Travel History', inspired and advanced my interests in, and understandings of, hotel history, as did those in several undergraduate classes, including 'Topics in Global History'. Many MA students whom I have had the privilege to advise also encouraged me to consider tourism and hotels in new ways: Shannon O'Connor, Monica Finlay, Chris Quinn, Erica German, Wade Cormack, Alex Clay, Jonathon Barraball, Evan Tigchelaar, Nick Bridges, Michael Postiglione, Fergus Maxwell and Brad Larkin. Undergraduate research assistants Matthew Midolo and Brad Larkin worked assiduously in identifying valuable sources for this book. Postdoctoral scholar Eddie Rogers assisted in conceptualising elements of the project. My professional collaborations and personal interactions with Patrick Vincent and Laurent Tissot of the Université de Neuchâtel have enabled me to develop a deeper appreciation of the European hotel, and my editorial and scholarly collaborations with Eric G.E. Zuelow of the University of New England have been immensely fruitful. John K. Walton provided early encouragement for my research into hotel histories which set me on this path one decade ago. The hotel scholars A.K. Sandoval-Strausz, Daniel Maudlin, Maurizio Peleggi, Cédric Humair and Molly Berger participated in a roundtable for the *Journal of Tourism History* that offered insight into hotel history. Britta Hentschel engaged in a valuable virtual discussion in my graduate classes, as did Molly Berger and Mathieu Narindal. Bob Davidson and Eric Jennings shared research with our class during our explorations of hotel history. These scholars have helped me to develop a deeper grasp of the modern hotel's complex history. I am very grateful to all of them.

Institutional support from the University of Guelph, where I have also enjoyed friendship and encouragement from colleagues including Tara Abraham, Andrew Bailey, William Cormack, Peter Eardley, Peter

Goddard, Rüdiger Mueller and Jesse Palsetia, helped bring this book to fruition. The Tourism History Working Group at the University of Guelph, including colleagues Linda Mahood and Alan Gordon, provided a collegial forum for sharing ideas. Bob Davidson supplied me with a draft of his book in advance of its publication. He, as Director of the Northrop Frye Centre at the University of Victoria College at the University of Toronto, and staff and scholars there, provided great company, insight and a delightful environment in which to complete revisions to this work in 2018, through a Visiting Fellowship. Mark Young at the Hospitality Archives, Hilton College, University of Houston, identified, from a distance, many images for this book, and the Harry Ransom Centre at the University of Texas at Austin also supplied research support and a congenial site for research and writing through a Research Fellowship supported by the Andrew W. Mellon Foundation Research Fellowship Endowment. I am grateful for the generous use of images from sources acknowledged in this book.

Channel View Publications has been a great pleasure to work with, at all levels and stages of this book's development, and the kindness and patience shown to me by editor Sarah Williams is much appreciated, as is the encouragement of the editors of the Tourism and Cultural Change series, Mike Robinson and Alison Phipps. Extensive comments provided through the process of anonymous peer review were constructive and helped to tighten the focus of this study: I am very grateful for perceptive remarks supplied in detail, with a view to improvement.

Monica Rieck has been a supporter of this book, and all of my other research projects, as my wife and best friend: she has read it in several versions, some very preliminary, and I thank her for helping me to revise and realise it. Our son Charles and daughter Helen have developed a new appreciation for hotels, a fondness for tourism history that almost matches their keenness for travel itself, and a capacity to share their enthusiasm for new places, as well as an openness to new perspectives on those places, that inspires me. My parents, Joseph James and Jane Marie James, and my brother Michael and his family have also been great sources of support. My Nana, the late Helen M.N. McNab, always encouraged my interests in History.

All errors and omissions in this study are my own. Many of what I believe to be its best elements are due to conversations involving the many people mentioned above. I am very grateful to them for their support of this project.

1 Introduction

This book surveys key themes in the historiography of the urban, Western hotel. Its focus is the current state of the field of hotel history – examining scholarship that largely treats the hotel within realms, such as Europe and America, and within frameworks, such as colonialism and globalisation, that are associated with advanced capitalism, Western political hegemony and cultural and economic modernity. Scholars over many generations have tended to regard the hotel as a pre-eminently modern institution. It incubates innovation and incorporates and exports cutting-edge technology. It fosters styles of sociability integral to highly networked, urban and advanced industrial societies, enables intensive commercial relations on a variety of scales and supplies an arena for negotiating relations of political, cultural and economic power. In manifesting 'mobile' modernity, it undermines traditional systems of social management. It has become enfolded with a number of broader historical narratives, including three which are the focus of this book: (1) America's status as an innovator in technologies and services; (2) patterns of European colonialism and decolonisation; and (3) contours of violent conflict, especially against the backdrop of late 20th-century American hegemony and Europe's imperial retreat. These themes lie at the heart of this analysis of the hotel, including its inscriptional power, in a variety of historical settings.

Almost all scholars who turn their attention to hotels and their histories contend that hotels are uniquely embedded within the structures of modern life. They are a key part of many people's daily lives: as places of rest between periods of motion, hotels are networked into the rhythms of work and leisure. They recharge and pamper our tired bodies, provide space for celebrating key moments in our lives, supply sites for shopping, strolling and 'waiting' (Tallack, 2002), as well as moments of *frisson* and mundane encounters. Hotels play a role in shaping our sense of self and our social, economic, political and cultural affiliations and identities. They also occupy a central role in popular culture, from novels to horror films to television shows (Murphy, 2014). Hotels' physical properties, especially their mix of private and public spaces, scaffold genres from comedy to mystery (Bayley, 2010: 91–124; Krebs, 2009). Cultural studies scholars have offered insights into dynamics of hotel life premised on the notion that hotels carry and shape shifting values, aspirations, dreams and desires (Levander & Guterl, 2015: i). They have attracted literary critics interested in their dramatic role in life writing, fiction, theatre and film (Ebert & Schmid, 2018; Fick, 2017). They have also been the subject of wide-ranging explorations and exhibitions that ambitiously synthesise their wider meaning (Volland & Grenvillle, 2013). As places of work and play, sociability and alienation, production and consumption, licence and surveillance, they are sites in which ambivalences associated with the modern condition are played out.

This book is designed as a primer on hotel scholarship that underlines and explores the remarkably fruitful exchanges between historians and social scientists, initially primarily in the realm of applied scholarship, and now increasingly within the contexts of critical cultural studies and humanities scholarship. The proliferation of such studies provides the context for this book's survey of, and critical engagement with, a number of their claims. Historical perspectives have figured prominently in the Tourism and Cultural Change series, often through concerns with heritage (Conlin & Bird, 2014; Xie, 2015) – ways in which the past is narrated and commodified for tourist consumption, and how particular tourist sites are produced through systems of signification (Waterton & Watson, 2014). Three titles in the series have a primary historical focus: Peter Borsay and John K. Walton's (2011) collection on the evolution of European resorts and ports, which embraces the diverse functions of the urban seaside, Betty Hagglund's (2010) study of travel writing on Scotland and John K. Walton's (2005) landmark collection *Histories of Tourism: Representation, Identity and Conflict*. The latter collection stands out as one of the earliest efforts to supply a forum for the exchange of scholarly perspectives in a field that Walton pioneered. Although this book's goal is to supply a critical survey of hotel history scholarship, like other titles in the Tourism and Cultural Change series, this book is interested in tourist sites, their signification and their participation in the symbolic and material economies of tourism. The hotel, however, stands outside conventional understandings of many tourist sites, and demands separate analysis. It is part of the infrastructure of travel, conventionally understood and studied as a place of rest, not of motion. It is integral to the consumption of tourist space in complex ways that raise questions as to whether it is part of, or a refuge from, the realm through which one travels – a place of the extraordinary, the mundane, or an intersection of the two.

The hotel is a creature of culture, and develops a culture of its own. Importantly, the hotel's economic networks, cultural position and political roles extend far beyond the tourism economy, which is the focus of most books in this series. Part of this book's aim is to show where tourism figures into narratives of the hotel, especially after 1800, to identify the hotel's other functions, and its other 'users' – among them commercial travellers, long-term hotel residents, colonial administrators, the wartime press and armed combatants. In exploring the hotel as a cultural object, this apprises readers of important new research in a dynamic field of tourism scholarship. It explores how commercial accommodation has become a key concern of historians, and how they have drawn from a broad range of disciplines, theoretical apparati and evidence as the field of hotel history has matured. Departing from the potted, descriptive hotel history narratives that occupy comparatively small space in hospitality management text books, and the theoretical orientation of cultural studies of the hotel, it identifies three specific areas of empirical research, as an introduction to exploring how historians have handled hotels as institutions, drawing on the insights of sociologists, political scientists, architectural historians and others. All three research agendas are concerned with the hotel's inscriptional power, and with relationships between spatial regimes and sociabilities. All treat the hotel as a political and cultural bellweather – of urban dynamism, of the condition of broader economic networks, and of civic and civil stability. And all tend to impute a set of defining, shared characteristics among the broad range of establishments that constitute institutional types, with coherent histories and identities – the 'American hotel', the 'colonial hotel' and the 'wartime hotel'. This book engages with these claims, using case studies and charting evolving perspectives on hotel history in these areas of scholarship:

(1) The first line of enquiry examines how scholars have charted the emergence of a unique, American institutional form, characterised by distinctive features in comparison with the European hotel, such as a comparatively high level of technologisation, and recent global sectoral dominance.
(2) The second line of enquiry explores how scholars have approached the functions of the European hotel in transmitting technologies, mediating cultural contact and producing hybridised cultural and social forms in colonial and postcolonial contexts.
(3) The third and final line of enquiry analyses how students of the urban hotel have treated its embroilment within the ideological and tactical dynamics of armed conflict, often engaging with biopolitics.

When this book refers to a hotel as an 'inscribed place', it denotes ways in which its meaning is produced and reproduced, contested and reconfigured over time, by people and institutions engaged in its creation – those who design, finance and build it – as well as ways that it has been mediatised, and how it has been used, or 'consumed'. The book traces the history of a number of establishments, and several institutional constructs – such as the American hotel – whose discursive positioning and repositioning over time reflects the shifting power of particular class, cultural and political interests and reveals conflicts among them as the meanings of hotels and the wider places they inhabit are contested and change. These processes by which the built form is subject to conflicting inscriptions and enrolled within debates are rendered most visible when hotels are physically destroyed or radically repurposed. Hotels can be 'read' as manifestations of these, and more subtle, contentious inscribing and re-inscribing processes that reconfigure them materially and symbolically. Their relationship to their wider ecologies, such as the urban landscape, can also be studied in terms of the hotel's own inscriptional power: its physical form (such as height and design), location (in an area in which particular buildings, institutions, or populations are concentrated), relationship to other institutions, and functions and ways that it is inhabited (and by whom) as an institution. These considerations encompass how it orders commerce, sociability and political administration. Architectural historians and cultural geographers have offered piercing insights into these processes. This book invites readers to consider how hotels' meanings were erected along with buildings, how they evolved, were contested and often reconfigured.

Across the strands of hotel history that it explores, this book underlines the implications of the hotel's relative 'openness' to its wider environment. In America, the hotel's metaphorical openness to the street was seen as a defining feature of the institution, to the extent that it absorbed and even began to order the public sphere. In colonial realms, the hotel has been treated not as an insular, closed vessel of metropolitan culture, but rather as a porous, hybridised space, expressed not only in its architecture, but also in complex social interactions that it fostered. Even more baldly, in conflict zones, the hotel's comparative openness has often made it a 'soft target' – as well as an institution susceptible to repurposing in the prosecution of war. Some degree of porousness is seen as essential to the fundamental institutional identity of the hotel: indeed, it is a cardinal requirement for the provision of hospitality. Though it is neither wholly public nor wholly private, and access to various spaces is hierarchically organised and conditioned by socio-economic status, gender and race, the hotel's openness has historically made it permeable, adaptive and vulnerable.

Framing the hotel as an open, Western and modern institution has consequences for the narration of commercial accommodation's history generally and forms of hospitability with which they have been associated. They are often grafted onto a teleological narrative of the hotel's modernity and its key role in ordering sociability. Primary sources, the historian's building blocks, offer evidence of this emplotment. Correspondence and reports in the pages of the British hospitality trades' journal, *Caterer, Hotel Keeper and Restaurateur's Gazette*, for example, charted the hotel's development within a narrative of progress that heaped praise upon visionary leaders of the sector and lauded innovative technologies adopted in the great hotels of the West, which were then exported to all four corners of the world. Ruminations on the modern hotel were often expressed in wistful, romantically infused portrayals of the inn of 'bygone days'. Take this example from the 16 May 1898 issue:

> How delightful it is at the end of a long ride or tramp over rough roads to enter the snug bar-parlour of one of those charming old country inns, now, alas! growing year by year more rare. How pleasant to stretch one's tired limbs in a comfortable arm-chair. There is a certain cosiness about these old inn sitting rooms to be found nowhere else except, possibly, in the kitchen of some ancient farmhouse. The red curtains, the saw-dusted floor, the beam-crossed ceiling, dusky with the smoke of generations, the long wooden tables and oaken settles form a delightful whole. The hostess bustles about intent on your comfort. You feel rather as if you were an honoured guest than a mere stranger who pays his bill and goes on his way. How great is the contrast to the huge modern hotel, where you are lost in a crowd, your individuality swamped, and yourself only known by a number. Long may they flourish, these fine old country inns, for truly no more essentially English institution yet remains with us. (232)

Many nostalgic appraisals of the English inn that extolled its unique charms venerated an institution that materialised distinctive, indigenous hospitality. These narratives, boasting bucolic images (Figure 1.1), proliferated as the death-knell was rung for the small hostelry. That event was rhetorically cast as part of the inexorable rise of the large-scale hotel – a novel institution and a harbinger of new social relations of commercial hospitality.

This discourse and visual culture had counterparts elsewhere in Europe. The French *auberge*, the German *gasthaus*, the Danish *kro* and the Swiss mountain inn were seen as being deeply rooted in their

Figure 1.1 England, The Old Inn on village street in Widecombe-in-the-Moor, ca. 1934–1969

respective, rustic *terroirs*. Just as they manifested and preserved indigenous qualities, the inn, this essentialist narrative declared, was a vessel – perhaps *the* vessel – of English identity and tradition. Quintessentially English values and regimes of sociability were preserved under the roof of a building whose scale fostered intimacy, and whose aesthetic was as timeless and as familiar as the fare offered by the hands of welcoming hosts. Readers were invited to snuggle vicariously into the inglenook over warm beer, and to share stories with fellow guests and with the innkeeper beside the roaring fire – as far from the busy grand hotels' clerks' desks, grand dining rooms and capacious lobbies as could be imagined. And *imagination* is crucial here – for poles of sociability were co-constructed with the rural inn and the urban grand hotel, as these two types were identified with contrasting social regimes and physical properties – scales, aesthetics, labour forces, levels of technologisation and forms of personalised attendance. The familiarity and 'foreignness' of fare also supplied an index of indigenous institutions, the inn supplying 'known' dishes and the hotel more elaborate food and beverages, often with a foreign flourish.

This institutional–cultural difference was far more embedded than any legal distinction. Earlier in the 19th century, the Law of Innkeepers, an agglomeration of common and statute law, recognised the distinction between the inn and the hotel in purely functional terms: the inn supplied travellers and other casual guests, along with their horses, with food and lodging. The hotel, a comparatively new term in law, supplied lodging only (Willcock, 1829: 1). By the mid-Victorian era this functional difference had dissolved, although the idea of the inn as a site of distinctively intimate conviviality endured – it was a place that was resistant to the metropolitanism and cosmopolitanism signified by the grand hotel.

The urban grand hotel, pre-eminently America's 'palace' variety, attracted sustained attention from journalists, social commentators and – from the first decades of the 20th century – sociologists who saw it as a central component of the modern urban landscape and of the processes which produced it: industrialisation, urbanisation, commercial capitalism and the development of especially dynamic civic identities and political cultures. As a creature of modernity, its combination of technological advancement, spatial organisation and divisions of labour engendered scepticism over the hotel's capacity to foster meaningful social interaction. Western hotels also invited mediations on the implications of industrial capitalism's consolidation, urban life, technology, the extension of Western political authority, the global diffusion of Western capital and the movement of travellers in large numbers into the farthest corners of the world. Observing how the hotel seemed to enable rapid circulations of people, resources and ideas, some observers surmised that regimes of control and even coercion operated behind the hotel's revolving doors, however much the frenetic pace of activity seemed to impede and defy them. Others saw the hotel as a place of almost painful anomie and alienation. The familiar inn, by contrast, slipped into a trite rendering of Pickwickian hostelries and Falstaffian companionability in a proliferating number of nostalgic texts.

The Urban Milieu

By surveying histories of the Western – and particularly the British and American – hotel at home and abroad, and by identifying how it has been explored in narratives of economic, social and cultural modernisation, this book underscores the primacy accorded to the urban milieu and to the grand hotel form – and indeed adopts that focus in its critical examination of hotel history. Hotel history tends to naturalise the hotel as an urban creature. The oft-cited metaphor of a 'city within a city' potently expressed the embeddedness of hotel 'life' within the late-19th-century urban milieu, and suggested that the hotel replicated the density of the urban world, internalised its intensity and diversity, and elaborated its logic. It became a microcosm of the modern urban landscape with which it was pre-eminently associated.

Studying the hotel in urban America, in the urban contexts of European colonialism, and in circumstances of urban-based, violent conflict allows us to interrogate ways in which the hotel was inhabited and itself inhabited urban space. In America, the palace hotel was hailed as the supreme expression of a vigorous capitalist ethos anchored by an emerging urban system. It was regarded as the iconic signifier of a putatively new and more democratic public culture than that which was represented by the staid and stolid grand hotels of the continent, and it played a key role in fashioning and stabilising social relationships, civic identities and political spaces. Hotels were seen as integral to the commercial and political dynamism of the nation. Old World hotels were said to bear the markers of the socially exclusive realms of the aristocratic abode, and hence they were regarded as intrinsically unconducive to creating a demotic, American-style 'public square'. At the same time, as one of the hotel's most perceptive chroniclers, A.K. Sandoval-Strausz, reminds us, while Americans erected a new state, with a distinctive civic culture, the hotel became central to the logic of spatial–social management, through strategies of 'exclusion and compartmentalisation' that were enacted within the microspaces of these palaces of the public (Sandoval-Strausz, 2007: 36). In Europe's colonial realms, where the grand hotel was often among the most prominent buildings in the landscape, the institution frequently boasted a bewildering aesthetic pastiche that signalled how its spaces, rather than instantiating the *métropole*, were sites of hybridity, contest, conflict and mediation. Here an aura of social exclusivity was often infused with a remarkable cultural heterogeneity at all levels, signalling its status as a site of encounter – and as a nerve-centre networking capital and people in the colonial enterprise.

The hotel's capacities to structure such flows, rather than merely serve as a conduit for them, is a critical consideration here. As Robert A. Davidson (2006: 169) argues in a case study of the Catalan hotel as a vessel for the transmission of architectural and cultural styles, hotels organise the diffusion of goods, people, behaviour, styles and aesthetics in nuanced ways. Those means of transmission, and the scales of the networks through which they are transmitted, are of particular interest to hotel historians. It is easy to assume that colonial hotels were mere metropolitan appendages, catering to Western tastes, ordering commerce and sociability, and signifying Western hegemony. Indeed, such an interpretation fits comfortably with the grand narrative of the 'rise' of the metropolitan hotel. It charts the hotel's inexorable expansion and global diffusion through which an essential metropolitan hotel form became a monument and marker of Western culture and global capitalism. But, as this book shows, scholars have unpacked complex colonial and postcolonial hotel histories that defy this interpretation of the hotel as a metropolitan transplant.

One particular hotel form – the grand hotel – has been studied by scholars interested in its functions and forms in spatial networks operating on a number of scales (local, regional, national, transnational and also in the context of de-territorialised actors and networks, such as terrorist organisations). In American scholarship, the palace hotel has been studied as both a local and translocal institution (Sandoval-Strausz, 2007: 76). In colonial milieus, grand hotels were knitted into local as well transnational networks (King, 2016). Western travellers in colonial realms were attracted to, and intrigued by, the hotel's interpolations of the old and the new, and the unfamiliar and the familiar – hinted at by pastiche interior and exterior ornamentation and by hybridised architectural forms. Hotels also provided critical physical affordances – windows, balconies and verandas – which framed and structured landscapes and people outside its walls, illustrated by Figure 1.2, which shows a view of late-19th-century Tunis from the Paris Hotel, the gaze structured 'above' the colonial city. They could also shape gazes from the outside *into* the hotel (Goh, 2010: 181). Gazes that were often directed 'above' old cities from vantage-points in hotels were also structured in rural environments, where nature was framed in ideologically freighted ways through the material affordances of hotel space. Figure 1.3 shows the Buffalo Mountains in the colony of Victoria, now part of Australia, as seen from the Eurabin Hotel, which casts the eye upwards towards the mountains. Prospects above mountains, canyons, waterfalls and other natural features trained the eye on them in ways that shaped subjective experiences in relation to both the spaces of the hotel and of nature, and became deeply involved in processes through which landmark sites and views were configured and mediatised. At the same time, metropolitan hotels were influenced by the aesthetics, and even the cuisine, of empires. With their exotically decorated public rooms, plumed décor and colourful cocktails, they offered an entrée into the colonial realm through their own doors, configuring the consumption of empire at home.

In addition to examining scholarly treatments of American and colonial grand hotels, this book explores scholarship on hotels as institutions

Figure 1.2 General view from Paris Hotel, Tunis, Tunisia, ca. 1899

Figure 1.3 The Buffalo Mountains from Eurabin Hotel, published 1886

operating within contexts of urban violence, examining how and why they were targeted and inhabited and how they operated. Hotels have conventionally been defined as 'soft targets' of terrorism, in the lexicon of security studies. Scholars underline their high vulnerability, alongside other relatively public urban spaces such as shopping malls and churches. A distinctive logic assigns use-values to hotels in areas of violence, according to the priorities of combatants. In the context of continuous armed conflicts between identified belligerents, the conquest of the hotel is often a tactical priority. In a terrorist campaign, it can supply a target where damage can be inflicted on a concentrated population. Sometimes the commercial functions of the hotel persist in wartime, defying the disorderly world around it. Its operations continue while many other institutions and sectors are profoundly disrupted. Guests and employees might maintain (often privileged) access to resources within the hotel's (often fortified) boundaries, which reinforce its status as an island amid a sea of violence and disarray – but this also 'de-territorialises' it in ways that make it vulnerable to framing as a 'foreign' site that 'occupies' space around it. At other times, the urban hotel's functions are severely disrupted, and it is adapted for uses that are integral to the prosecution and resolution of armed conflict, from supplying advantageous vantage-points for snipers, to headquartering the bureaucracy of war, to hospital facilities for the wounded, to sites of conflict mediation. When hotels were historically targeted, the dynamics of hostilities starkly revealed both their inscriptional power and ways in which they were symbolically enrolled within conflicts – sometimes signifying imperialism, sometimes capitalism, sometimes both – making their 'conquest' symbolically potent, as well as materially advantageous. Hotel spaces were contested, and their operations and meanings were reconfigured through violence.

What is a Hotel?

This survey of scholarship invites readers to ask how hotel histories are structured and told. It critically explores conventional accounts of the institutions' histories, and examines how specific similes and metaphors organise explanations of the hotel – as a machine, for example, as a living creature, or, as we have seen, as a 'city' in its own right. It underlines the frequent organic narrative of the 'birth' and 'death' of establishments, and its implications for how we conceive of the 'natural' experiences – of institutional forms and of particular establishments – as we plot and read their histories. Hotel histories often adopt a teleology that occludes the imbrication of institutional types. It is tempting to assume that the label describes an essential institutional form, though the term designated many forms of commercial hospitality in different places and in historical periods. Indeed, some scholars trace the Western hotel's genealogy back to Ancient Greece and Rome, through medieval monasteries to 18th-century hostelries (Firebaugh, 1972; MacDonald, 2000; O'Gorman, 2009). John K. Walton (2014: 1039) has also helpfully reminded us that although the term now is used interchangeably with a range of institutions, there was an important historical distinction between a hotel and a spa, which was associated with 'medicinal use of mineral springs', and a resort, which denoted a 'location (anything from a hotel or village to a whole town or even city) where people congregate in search of health, recreation and pleasure'.

This imprecision in nomenclature has a long pedigree. Nineteenth-century records in Britain especially elicit little clarity or agreement on the definition of a hotel. As Lisa Pfueller Davidson (2005a) persuasively argues, the taxonomy of commercial accommodation was decidedly imprecise, and the meaning of 'hotel' unsettled, in the 19th century. The designation 'hotel' was adopted by a variety of establishments that might now be recognised as diverse institutional types (Davidson, 2005a: 115). This unsettled terminology partly reflects the relatively recent assimilation of the term within the English language, its first documented use being in the late 18th century (Pevsner, 1976: 172). It initially had functional connotations, rather than supplying a descriptor for a specific building type (Sandoval-Strausz, 2007: 6). A.K. Sandoval-Strausz (2007: 7) contends that the architectural category developed simultaneously in Britain, the cradle of industrialisation, and in republican America, which had thrown off the yoke of colonialism. By the later 19th century it began to describe a more consistent or uniform building, which was in turn identified with distinctive spatial arrangements, technological systems and urban environments. If, as Nikolaus Pevsner (1976) claims in his survey of public building typologies, the hotel's origins lay in both early modern continental spas and large-scale inns, the hotel's scale and its novel external and internal systems of operation were hallmarks of a new institution that lay at the heart of a correspondingly advanced 'hotel system': enormous, vital, mechanistic and synchronised. In the 19th century, the American hotel was often seen as its supreme institutional expression, signalled by its minute and efficient organisation of technologies and labour. This status was reflected not just by its size and operations, but also by the forms of sociability that it fostered. Commentators who held that the hotel was an outgrowth of urbanisation, industrialisation and commercial maturation also regarded it as a site in which a new and distinctively modern subjectivity was forged. Many located its most advanced example in a nation that had deliberately shaken off the yoke of Europe and its rigid social hierarchies, and which had developed institutions as novel as its civic spirit. The American hotel was often hailed, and sometimes denounced, as singular. The elaboration of an enduring binary between European and American hotel cultures had foundations in a hotel ontology articulated with power and persuasion by Henry James (1907) in his landmark sociological exploration of the 'hotel spirit' in America. The institution offered James a prism through which to explore the American culture, and draw stark comparisons with that of Europe. The later, interwar period also proved especially fertile for scholars of the hotel – supplying not only one of the most influential meditations on the hotel as a locus of modern sociability in Siegfried Kracauer's Weimar essays (2004), but also a landmark study of the American hotel by Norman S. Hayner (1936). Soaring urban palace and grand hotels were laboratories to dissect the conditions of modern urban life. As we shall see in Chapter 3, Hayner explicated hotel life in relation to the social regimes of the modern American city, arguing that particular demographic, social and economic structures shaped Americans' distinctive relationship to their hotels. The hotel was integral to the structures of urban life and urban living – an institution inextricably tied to patterns of modernisation which involved the aggregation of capital, the specialisation of labour and innovations in technology and design. Their implications were evident in social relations that were enacted in its lobbies, corridors and private rooms. The ways the urban hotel's spaces were inhabited, to Kracauer and Hayner, whether in Berlin or in New York, epitomised aspects of the modern condition – and often tended towards alienation.

Modern Hotel History Scholarship

In more recent decades, two broad waves of scholarship within hotel history have emerged, outside a primarily biographical literature which has focused on figures associated with the founding and management of particular establishments and chains (e.g. Lee, 1985). One of these waves has been commemorative, and can be understood in the context of a current of nostalgia for particular, putatively 'dying' or 'lost' hotel forms. The metaphors of life and death became especially potent in narrations of the grand hotel's experience, and their profusion in print coincided with the apparent, irreversible decline of conditions that marked the hotel's rise, from the eclipse of the railway to the dismantling of colonialism. Suburbanisation, the advent of the automobile, the expansion of the multinational chain and decolonisation all seemed to herald the end not only of the grand hotel, but also of the social, economic, cultural and political contexts in which it emerged (Kramer, 1978). Its chronicles often took the form of glossy institutional histories in coffee-table book format (Donzel *et al.*, 1989; Frischauer, 1965; Montgomery-Massingbred & Watkin, 1980) implicitly or explicitly eulogising the grand hotel's 'golden age' (Taylor & Bush, 1974), and contrasting it to new travel cultures – and new constituencies of travellers. They sought to capture the aura and mystique of the grand hotel in vivid colour and exuberant prose. These surveys incorporated a substantial source base, including architectural records and building images, but their approach was often uncritical, and occasionally their tone proclaimed nostalgia not only for the old hotel, but for the old social codes and social mores, as well as for the old political systems (including colonialism) that were seen as critical to sustaining their vibrancy. Not all institutional biographies have been written in this vein: Nadja Maillard's collection *Beau-Rivage Palace: 150 Years of History* (2008) seeks to place the history of a building, produced on a commemorative occasion, within a critical frame. Others became part of a programmatic effort to build a heritage brand by expounding the history of an institution. Many narratives offered requiems for a past age in a celebratory, if wistful, strain. Consider Michel de Grèce's foreword to a lavishly illustrated tome on the (tellingly-named) 'Oriental Hotel' type. Perhaps befitting the scion of a family whose circumstances bore witness to the decline of aristocratic power in much of continental Europe, he struck an elegiac note, echoing a lament that has become a trope in many such histories: that the modern hotel guest was little more than a number to hosts:

> [t]here is no doubt that the great Oriental palaces have lost their lustre. Much of their sumptuous and old world charm have largely disappeared, and their mystery is nearly dead. By definition, the palaces are grand hotels; and today, all over the world, they are tending to become impersonal, dehumanised factories in which the guest is only another number ... And yet, despite the slow decay that we call progress, beneath the surface, the Palaces of the Orient still retain a part of their unpredictable quality, their romanticism, even their glamour. (de Grèce, 1987: 9)

Such accounts sounded a note of melancholy for a lost world as they extolled the romantic grand hotel aura and an era associated with an exclusive cadre of cultivated travellers, united by taste and exemplified by the genteel figures represented outside the Grand Hotel Khartoum in Figure 1.4. Here the underlying narrative was structured in relation to an appraisal of the contemporary hotel, and of the hospitality sector generally, as antiseptic and mundane, the culture of travel connoisseurship having dissolved into a set of practices as demotic as chain hotel rooms were indistinguishable. The grand hotel, which begat a popular narrative genre that entertained and enthralled readers and cinemagoers in the interwar period, supplying touchstones in popular culture, was consigned to the past, alongside the vibrant culture that it nourished. Jean d'Ormesson restated Michel de Grèce's notes of *tristesse*, lamenting that: '[t]o speak of grand hotels is to speak of shades of yesteryear, of shrines to another era, of legendary havens for exotic travellers and exiles rich as Croesus, of ephemeral abodes for hedonists in pursuit of luxury and heavenly bliss, or, if you will, of the romance between wealth and poetry, of dwellings where sheer splendour carries the day in a frenzied modern world' (d'Ormesson, 1984: 7). This association of the hotel with a lost world of international cosmopolitanism suggests the decline of a coterie of elite travellers, and the displacement of travelling practices which sustained not only the institution, but a more ineffable, romanticised 'grand hotel life'.

Figure 1.4 European couple and an African man wearing a European suit and fez, in front of the Grand Hotel, Khartoum, n.d.

From this genre, if not from this particular intellectual stance, emerged a thoughtful survey of the grand hotel over a wide expanse of space and time, authored by Elaine Denby (1998). Drawing back the veil of mystique that was as heavy as the chintz drapery of the archetypal grand hotel, Denby employs an implicit organic narrative of birth, maturation and decline in her landmark account of the institution. Denby's survey situates the grand hotel within a continuum of types, and explores its various national manifestations and transnational diffusion. Denby's book is a ground-breaking study of the institution's functions and forms which other scholars have queried, modified and challenged in theoretically grounded case studies. Indeed, the publication of Denby's study marked an important advancement towards greater analytic engagement with the hotel as an historical subject. This was accompanied by: (1) increasing interest in the historical dimensions of the hotel in applied tourism scholarship, in part because of the influence of models such as R.W. Butler's (1980) Tourism Area Life Cycle, which requires historical frames; and (2) the adoption of longitudinal lenses to explore transformations in the geography of commercial lodging, as part of the wider analysis of tourism's change over time (e.g. Rogerson, 2013; Shoval & Cohen-Hattab, 2001). In fact, longitudinal analyses of the lodging sector constitute ways through which historical sources and approaches have been incorporated within critical scholarship, especially through historical geography.

Another scholarly area whose practitioners have adopted a distinctive historical orientation, especially from the 1980s, is hotel sociology, which has often aimed to explicate 'hotel culture' within historical coordinates. Sociology has, in many respects, 'led' many innovative directions in hotel history, nourishing an early 20th-century interest in delineating the evolution of the modern form, and deeply informing recent critical examinations of the institution's past, from social and spatial practices in American hotels, to the symbolic and material reconfigurations of hotels in the postcolonial era, to strategies of hotel securitisation in conflict zones. Historical processes have also been central to sociological explanations of the modern hotel as a site of particular configurations of social relations. Explorations of the historical relationships between the hotel and the home, for example, are salient to explaining the ways that class relations were handled within contemporary commercial lodgings (Fick, 2017). In Europe, the ethos of the grand hotel is often seen as replicating the domestic culture of the socio-economic elite. Indeed, Rob MacDonald (2000: 145) contends that the late-18th-century hotel was 'cross breeding of the inn with the country house'. In an important study, Michael Riley (1984) theorises that the modern hotel evolved as an extension of the domestic realm of powerful socio-economic groups (exemplified by its higher cuisine). Its historical coordinates became central to ways it was commodified. The hotel adopted markers of exclusiveness from the houses at which propertied travellers historically stayed. In the process, the hotel was firmly differentiated from the historical rustic cuisine and social regimes of the lower-status inn. Under these influences, the modern institution reproduced status distinctions associated with its clientele. Hotel culture replicated the status of the wealthy host, signalled by the sophistication of its cuisine, and also by a 'knowledge differential' through which hotels developed an ethos of exclusivity that rendered them inaccessible to other social groups in an entrenched symbolic economy (Riley, 1984). In Riley's interpretation, the grand hotel was no palace of democracy, but a place whose carefully constructed 'culture' erected firm boundaries that were defined as much by cultural as economic resources. These characteristics are perhaps most conspicuously manifested in contemporary castle hotels, whose guests seek to 'revive' modes of aristocratic hospitality within an historical building that has been adapted as a prestigious lodging (Horváth & Nagy, 2012).

Endorsing Riley's contention that the origins of hotels' culture were in the social and spatial practices of the 'aristocratic domicile' (Wood, 1994: 67), Roy C. Wood (1994) questions Riley and Rita Carmouche's (1980) interest in explicating why the grand hotel has persisted in servicing a clientele defined by exclusive economic and cultural capital. Instead, Wood (1994: 77) seeks to clarify the historical processes through which the working classes were incorporated within the cultures of commercial accommodation, with hotels serving as class institutions and 'agents of social control'. Wood pointed to the technologisation of the hotel environment as a means through which the hotel's 'proletarianisation' was mediated and contained. The historical incorporation of technology was central to patterning sets of behaviour in which host-guest and guest-guest segregation became more acute. From the 1920s, Wood contends, technology was incorporated within the hotel room as a means of demarcating spaces of habitation, and the ways in which they were to be inhabited. Guests were expected to conform to unwritten codes that were associated with specific technologies. Private spaces, for example, were marked by a proliferation of domestic amenities available within them. Technology was thus central to the process of 'domestication', which drew ever-sharper distinctions between the hotel's public and private spaces. The spatial matrix into which these technologies were mapped evolved as the hotel grew in complexity and in scale, comprising banquet rooms, lobbies, retail shops, sample rooms, employee and servant accommodation, cafeterias, tea-rooms and suites of various sizes. Wood argues that historical, entwined disciplinary processes of domestication and technologisation that were enacted over guests were as old 'as hotels themselves' (Wood, 1994: 78). He also stresses that constraints placed on guests by these systems of control were actively resisted: the proliferation of accommodation options, notably self-catering lodging, reflected a defiance of the pervasive spatial and behavioural disciplinary regimes from the boarding house to the grand hotel (this claim is ripe for investigation by scholars of the proliferation of 'home-based' and 'home-like' accommodation in the 'shared economy'). This branch of hotel sociology's primary category of analysis is social class, and Wood's adopts the lens of 'social control'. There are other frames of analysis that explore hotel spaces and stress how they can provide interstitial sites in which social, cultural and legal codes can be contested and undermined, as well as affirmed.

Social scientists continue to elaborate historical studies which incorporate historical analytic components. They have oriented historical hotel scholarship away from a focus on approaches such as case studies of firms and topics such as business organisation (Baum & Ingram, 1998; Baum & Mezias, 1992; Ingram, 1996), although the study of the firm and the wider economic history of tourism remain important ways in which the sector continues to be explored (e.g. Pope, 2001, 2000; Walton, 2014; Weiss, 2004). An intensified application of critical theory to the study of the contemporary hotel has marked the field over the past decade, nurtured by:

(1) theorists such as Edward Said, and approaches including semiotics, Orientalism, postcolonialism and postmodernism (e.g. Jameson, 1991; Levander & Guterl, 2015);
(2) interest in the hospitality and tourism sectors as a focus for critical as well as applied study, especially in the Western academy, manifested in critical 'tourism studies'. In contrast, applied concerns often predominate in countries where tourism studies are oriented towards supporting priorities and programmes of economic development;
(3) the spatial turn in geography and other disciplines, influenced by scholars such as Henri Lefebvre and Michel de Certeau, and performance theory, as developed by Erving Goffman and others; and
(4) literary and film studies which have focused attention on the genres in which hotels are key settings and actors, and posit that the hotel is central to cultural configurations of modernism (Matthias, 2004, 2006; Saloman, 2012).

The critical turn in hotel history has led to a revival of interest in the interwar scholarship of Siegfried Kracauer and in theorists exploring the intersections of spaces, sociabilities and politics of governance, such as Walter Benjamin and Michel Foucault. Theoretically rich hotel history, sitting at the intersection of these diverse disciplinary interests, has directed attention to how the meaning and identity of a hotel is produced, how the spaces of the hotel produce a syntax for social interaction, and how the hotel materialises that syntax, from its architectural design to its exterior embellishments to its internal organisation and 'management'. Contemporary scholarship explores what A.K. Sandoval-Strausz (2007: 4) in his study of the hotel as a 'social technology' identifies elegantly as essential 'dilemmas of inclusion, exclusion, freedom and control' which involve technologies, hotel owners, managers, staff, guests and legal codes, implicit social conventions, and ideologies of gender, class and race. For example, scholars have highlighted the historical role of female labour in the hotel (Hayes, 2014; MacKay, 2017; Wright, 2001), especially in the context of small-scale and 'frontier' institutions in a number of places, such as colonial Australia. Such studies reflect a deepening interest in identities that were shaped by, and challenged within, the spaces of the hotel. With spaces that straddled public/private domains, hotels could offer scope for experimentation, consolidation, and contestation of hierarchies of socio-economic status, gender and race.

The Hotel as an Icon of Modernity

Most of this critical scholarship, whether emerging from political science, historical geography, architectural history, cultural history, or another disciplinary berth, explores the hotel as what Bettina Matthias calls 'one of the key witnesses to, as well as the product of, major power-shifts in Western society in the late 19th and early 20th century', with hotels constituting 'capitalized spaces that do not acknowledge or reveal their capitalist foundation' (Matthias, 2006: 3). Hotel architecture reflects changing spatial and social functions characteristic of modernity, involving new configurations of 'public and private, anonymity and intimacy, function and ornamentation, seeing and being seen' (Matthias, 2006: 4). Within this frame, networks of mobility have become a core concern of hotel history, with the hotel functioning as a node in circuits of people, capital, information and information. The compasses of these circuits can vary, embracing local, national and global levels. In servicing this range of networks, hotels have supplied a critical physical infrastructure. Like another 'grounded' infrastructure of travel – the airport – the hotel organises and mediates access to them. It also functions, as Mimi Sheller and

John Urry argue (2006), both as a 'transfer point' and a place of intermittent movement, with its own performance codes. Theoretically sophisticated analyses of the hotel's position within systems of mobility and circulation treat it as a key ordering institution of modern capitalism, from the era of European colonialism to a present-day era of 'globalisation' (Goh, 2010; Peleggi, 2012).

The political economy of the hotel, therefore, has become a core scholarly interest. In America, regarded as a leading organiser of advanced industrial capitalism, the hotel was a critical infrastructure in local economic development. The history of 'Main Street', in which the hotel figures prominently, offers a template for a broader history of American urban capitalism which cements the hotel's critical roles in structuring social and economic identities and nourishing the country's civic and commercial ethos. Landmark studies (Berger, 2011; Fick, 2017; Sandoval-Strausz, 2007) contend that the American hotel lay at the heart of scientific and technological innovations, not only through mechanisation, but also through the era of early-20th-century Taylorist managerialism. After World War II, the multinational hotel corporation became a vessel for exporting ideologically-freighted consumerist ideals (Mentzer, 2010). It signalled the power of American-influenced service culture, too – exemplified by a training regime designed to codify and disseminate meticulously-designed protocols of employee-guest engagement that governed the minutiae of their encounters. If the history in developing an institutional brand had incipient stages in Europe, where César Ritz discovered the marketing power of his name in the 19th and early 20th centuries, innovations across the Atlantic Ocean are associated with Americans such as Ellsworth Milton Statler and Conrad Hilton. Annabel Wharton argues that American hotel culture was extended into Europe and the Middle East as Hilton hotels were constructed in such places as Cairo (Figure 1.5). She argues that the institution was 'literally "a little America"' in the urban hotel topography (treated here as the location, distribution and forms of lodgings in a given space), signalling the imposition of new relations of authority upon the landscape (Wharton, 2001: 1). In London, Barbara Czyzewska and Angela Roper (2017) argue that the Hilton inscribed American postwar power. Around the globe, stark reconfigurations of authority were reflected in the reduced prominence of European colonial-era hotels in former imperial realms, and even in metropolitan centres of Europe. They reflected the new Western hegemon's economic, political and cultural power.

An important dimension of these studies of the intersection of hotel history and political economy has been attention to the hotel's

Figure 1.5 The Nile Hilton in the 1950s

relationship to forms of Western capitalism, liberalism and the neoliberal order. Although hotels in such contexts are the focus of this book, there has been rich scholarship on commercial accommodation within non-capitalist, non-democratic European environments, East and West. In the Soviet Union, for example, the resort system was integrated within a culture that tended to the body and reproduced the discipline of the factory floor, to shape the 'perfect worker' in the command economy (Koenker, 2013). Within the strictures of the spa regime were affordances for entertainment, leisure and pleasure; another paradox was the development of large-scale tourist sites, sometimes in former hotels, in the context of a regime whose ideology condemned the *petit bourgeois* character of the service sector (Koenker, 2013: 79–80). As proletarian tourism evolved, these contradictions remained at the heart of Soviet tourism. In another authoritarian European state, Francisco Franco's Spain, hotel development was part of a wider programme designed to lure Europeans to the country as tourists, fortifying the economic foundations of the dictatorial state (Pack, 2006). These, and many other examples, serve as reminders of the hotel's complex place within politico-legal regimes outside the liberal Western order, and signify the embeddedness of hotels and resorts within specific political, cultural and economic contexts, defying claims about the essential, global character of particular forms.

In exploring the hotel as an inscribed institution that also has inscriptional power, the next chapter begins by surveying how the hotel has been handled within a burgeoning academic field. Chapter 3 explores treatments of the American hotel, especially its precocious technologisation, its unique position within urban civic life, and its role as a signifier of the country's status in the international order after World War II. Chapter 4 explores how the colonial hotel was networked into specific urban systems, regimes of political authority, symbolic structures, and circuits and flows of people, capital, information and identities across oceans. It also explores scholarship that identifies hotels' malleable symbolisms in postcolonial contexts, when 'heritage' offers the potential to inscribe new political salience in them. Chapter 5 surveys a vibrant new research agenda examining hotels in the context of terrorism and more conventional urban warfare. Hotels' locational features, their material forms and their symbolisms have made them important objects of study during processes of urbanisation, capitalist development, nation building and colonial expansion. Interest in the relationship between hotels and violence is nourished by an awareness of their contemporary prominence as sites of violence, of diplomacy and of refuge in places from Baghdad to Bali to Mumbai to Kabul. The hotel is variously seen as a 'soft target', an asset, a safe haven and a nerve-centre. The study of the wartime hotel condenses many current focuses in the field of hotel history. It also reinforces the urban orientation of hotel history: the result of this tendency is to occlude or reify other institutions. The concluding chapter of this survey explores the historiographical implications of studying the hotel primarily as an urban (and Western) form of modern commercial accommodation, outlines some potentially very fruitful lines of enquiry that are outside the scope of this book, and sketches some preliminary ideas that might promote an even more expansive and reflexive hotel history as the field continues to develop.

2 Hotel History: Interpretations and Approaches

A number of historical processes are regarded as preconditions for the hotel's emergence as a lodestar of Western modernity: maturing industrialisation, with high levels of labour differentiation, advanced mechanisms and capacities for aggregating and deploying capital, increasing urbanisation, rising incomes and demand for leisure amenities, technological innovation and commercial expansion. How did the hotel become so durably entrenched in a master narrative that (1) pinpoints its birth in the late-eighteenth and early-19th-century West, and links it to these developments; (2) identifies a distinctive trajectory in America; (3) charts the growth of its scale and the extension of its reach into other parts of the world; and (4) treats it as a citadel of Western capitalism and political authority? A brief review of the conventional narrative of hotel history illuminates its arc. It is followed by an exploration of how the hotel as an institution has been defined in relation to the 'home', which is a crucial consideration in American, colonial and conflict-zone hotel histories. It then proposes a condensed hotel typology designed to underscore the diversity of hotel forms according to specific criteria. A survey of key approaches to the study of Western, urban hotel histories concludes this chapter, and supplies a framework for understanding how American, colonial and wartime hotels have been examined.

The Nineteenth-Century Hotel

In an account that is often badly teleological in charting its development as an institution, the modern hotel emerged as a distinctive form of commercial accommodation in late 18th- and early 19th-century western Europe and America, where capitalist development was most advanced. In Europe, its origins are sometimes attributed to establishments connected to the major resort complexes which attracted health-seeking visitors and to lodgings that were networked into commercial and transport infrastructures, both of which evolved over centuries. Some scholars pinpoint the emergence of the prototype of the modern grand hotel neither in Great Britain, nor in the United States, but rather in later 18th-century continental Europe (Denby, 1998: 23–26). The scale of the institution had important links to an institution whose history is well documented: the early-modern spa (Borsay & Walton, 2011; Cossic & Galliou, 2006; Hembry, 1990; Hembry *et al.*, 1997; Walton, 2014). The requirements of the continental 'Grand Tourist' generated demand for expanded commercial accommodation at spas whose fashionable status, amenities and social tone demarcated them from others. The curative properties associated with their waters produced social and medical regimes that catered to a socially exclusive constituency. Accommodation was often of high quality, if limited. In the late 18th century, the growth of the middle class produced greater demand for spa facilities and a corresponding growth in the scale of lodgings. Historic spa districts witnessed the development of built environments dominated by hotels: indeed, the historic spa supplies us with an example of how new forms of commercial accommodation were constructed in close proximity to, and sometimes even overlaying, existing infrastructures (Walton, 2012). The extent of this spa network can be overstated: most, as Peter Borsay and John K. Walton (2011) remind us, were small, catering largely to local and regional markets, with accommodation that bore little resemblance to the 'proto-hotels' of larger national and international resorts. Moreover, the network of inns that emerged with Europe's extensive road network, supporting trade, pilgrimage and other activities, although not always corresponding to the geography of hotel development in the 19th century, cannot be dismissed in favour only of resorts as the sole incubators of the hotel system; hence Rob MacDonald (2000) contends that both the inn and the country house exerted influence over the scale and culture of the hotel. MacDonald reminds us, as hotel sociologists have done, that the hotel bore the imprint of those two institutions.

The hotel was distinguished from preceding forms of commercial accommodation, such as the inn and the tavern, and from other medical and leisure institutions, such as the spa, by a number of characteristics, notably its scale and location, as well as the extent to which new technology became integral not only to its construction, but also to its internal operations. It was firmly embedded within networks of travel in an era marked by more extensive movement than ever before. In this interpretation of hotel development, the expansion of the hotel's functions were enabled by several factors, including (1) increased traffic across greater distances of travel; (2) new leisure and work practices associated with the rhythms of industrial society, including discrete periods of leisure and more extensive commercial travel; (3) new mechanisms for capital investment, such as the limited liability company; and (4) technological innovations in transport that disrupted and displaced infrastructures of travel and accommodation and produced a new geography of commercial accommodation.

In explicating the relationship between technologies of transport, forms of mobility and the hotel's development, the railway has been seen as *the* decisive influence over the 'birth' of the modern hotel (e.g. Simmons, 1984). Indeed, Elaine Denby (1998: 23) describes steam locomotion as the 'single most powerful catalyst' in the development of the institution. An early chronicler of the seaside hotel contends that '[i]t would be near the truth to suggest that the railways were the influence most responsible for the forms taken by hotel architecture in the last century' (Lindley, 1973: 80). The prevailing narrative of the hotel's development marries histories of transport and commercial lodging, and identifies the railway as the critical determinant of locational preferences, of traffic flows, and of sources, levels and organisations of capital that were conditions for the erection of a hotel topography. Steel and steam are presented as 'grounding' a new infrastructure for travel, resulting in a new geography of leisure and business travel, and new enterprises with capital and incentives for investment in commercial accommodation. Even *Chambers's Encyclopaedia* (1875: 436–437) in the 19th century insisted that the new institution of 'hôtel' had displaced the inn as a consequence of the new means of transport. The focus of such accounts has been primarily on elucidating the relationship between steam technology, railway networks and the development of hotel networks, yet pleasure steamers and railway sleeping cars reproduced many of the features of the hotel. Closer attention to early ways in which these accommodation forms were networked within other public and private spaces in ways that resembled the bricks-and-mortar hotel (before, for example, the modern pleasure cruise), would repay attention. Indeed, in Martina Krebs's (2009: 24–34) analysis, the railway carriage and the ship are treated as 'moving hotels'. Instead, the evolution of the hotel's modern forms has been largely charted in relation to innovations in locomotion in which mechanical power displaced that of the sentient being – a process replicated in the hotel by the substitution of innovative labour-saving devices, which has obvious epistemological grounding in teleological narratives of the Industrial Revolution. More than a century later, that remains the predominant view of the hotel. In short, the histories of railway transport and modern commercial accommodation have been treated as inextricably entwined.

The advancement of the European grand hotel, and the adoption of its template farther afield, has been seen as marking a decisive break with the scale, service and 'hospitality cultures' of the past, albeit, as we have seen, perpetuating the culture and appointments of the aristocratic domicile. They heralded industrial Europe's hotel age – a period in which establishments expanded in size, scope of service and sophistication, extending their reach across oceans and into colonial environments. As the grand hotel's pre-eminent chronicler, Elaine Denby (1998) contends, during its heyday, which she dates from 1830 to the 1930s, the grand hotel assumed an unprecedented scale and cultural salience. David Watkin (1984: 18–19) concurs, charting the expansion of a 'Franco-American' type in 1870s Europe, but noting that despite their proliferation, such establishments generally lacked the 'architecturally festive' features and forms that prevailed during the heyday of the grand hotel from the 1880s to the 1920s. The era of opulent grand hotel culture, it is alleged, was prolonged in remote outposts of empire, which were marked by a rarefied European elite cosmopolitanism during the interwar period.

Elaine Denby sees transnational networks as crucial to the emergence of grand hotel culture – and underscores the extent to which the grand hotel was a materialisation of their influences, as emigrants from France (and later Switzerland) played a key role in exporting the type beyond the borders of their home country (Denby, 1998: 26). Grand hotels were not identical across borders and oceans. They carried the imprint of regional and national histories – and reflected distinctive, historical paths of economic and social development. But the grand hotel is regarded as a creature common to advanced, Western, industrial economies – America, Britain and northern Europe especially (rather than poorer southern and eastern European states). Switzerland's geography, location, popularity, fashionable status, political stability and the financial acumen of the sector's pioneers, along with prospects for social mobility there, incubated what Denby identifies as a distinctive Swiss hotel culture. It was marked as much by the concentration of first-class hostelries as by a programmatic system of *hôtellerie* that was unrivalled in Europe and the world – and became institutionalised in hotel training schools in the later 19th century (Denby, 1998: 111–135).

In charting distinctive national forms of the hotel, Denby argues that Great Britain's grand hotel boom went hand-in-hand with industrialisation, and thus was bound to its precocious economic development. England's railway hotels supplied a template that was ambitiously expanded north into Scotland, where the grand hotel took root in rural districts – often as part of an expansive leisure facility in which it was the predominant attraction, as well as the principal building. This regional variation has been highlighted by one of tourism's ablest social historians, Alastair J. Durie. Durie, along with James Bradley and Marguerite Dupree (2006), has illustrated how in Scotland a particular institutional type emerged – the hydro – drawing on a set of ideas about water therapy (hydropathy) that produced a range of purpose-built hotels, with many ventures from the 1860s operating on the limited liability principle. Through vicissitudes that marked the hotel sector generally, they adopted new functions, as part of a network of places which were characterised by a middle-class 'social tone' above that of the family hotel. They, like resorts and hunting lodges, were arenas through which patrons indulged not only in recreation and leisure, but also in social identity production and reproduction. These places of commercial accommodation, which were large in scale and often became a dominant part of the landscape (Calvert & Lambert, 1997), serve as stark reminders to us that the grand hotel, even in one of Europe's most urbanised countries, was not exclusively an urban creature, and that the 'hotel' was both an adaptive form and a malleable marker.

As in many other places, as purpose-built hotel accommodation expanded, it added to an inventory of commercial accommodation servicing different markets. The seaside boasted grand establishments of their own, from the towns of the English coast to American resorts such as Atlantic City (Thomas & Snyder, 2005). In catering to a mixed population of holiday-makers, and with an existing built environment, private homes often adapted to meet the requirements of travellers – seaside boarding houses, for example. The grand hotel, in the same resorts, serviced other commercial and leisure markets. While the railway is seen as the critical technology that produced the geography of the modern hotel, there are exceptions. In London, the construction of a number of illustrious establishments, including the famous Langham, was not a direct product of the mid-19th-century railway boom. The hotel's diffusion in the United Kingdom involved adaptation, mutation and myriad scales, markets and relationships to built and natural environments.

The continental European grand hotel's development was grounded in historical cultures of travel and networks of hostelries. In France, for example, the role of railway capital was less decisive (Denby, 1998: 84). It is surprising, given the debt owed to French nomenclature, and also given the prominent place accorded that country's grand hotels in pioneering the style in Europe, that, as Patrick Harismendy (2016) notes, the institution in France has no legal definition. In Germany, Denby argues that grand hotels emerged more directly from the old spa hotels (Denby, 1998: 95). Habbo Knoch (2008: 144–145) postulates that divergent hotel development in America and on the continent is explained by different historical structures of leisure, infrastructures and social practices. Knoch (2008: 144–145) argues that continental Europe's hotel culture was more heavily influenced by resort and spa culture in the later 19th century. Knoch endorses the view that the American hotel's distinctive urban topography and institutions manifested a 'republican and anti-aristocratic tradition' through a relatively greater 'public' nature. They signalled important differences in the hotel's participation in the symbolic language of civic engagement. In Europe, the historical influences of spa and resort culture articulated links to urbanity through a distinctive set of discourses and practices centred on particular constructions of 'lifestyle' by providing an institutional framework that linked elite culture in the town and countryside. Hotels aimed at an urban market by promoting integration between the two realms. Britons, hailing from the most urbanised and industrialised of the large European countries, found places of congregation in American hotels unfamiliar, and also encountered continental hotels as places of strange social conventions, not least the *table d'hôte*. Initially they recoiled at a practice adopted later in the 19th century in Britain, whereby hotel guests assembled at an appointed hour to dine in each other's company, with a set number of courses, choosing from among a range of options (Mullen & Munson, 2010: 268–273). To contemporaries, American, continental and British hotels were different creatures. Hotel historians have tended to endorse that view by charting their parallel, distinctive trajectories.

The hotel's development was influenced by legal systems, levels of capitalist development, prospective markets and the character of historical accommodation networks and cultures, as well as by indigenous architectural styles, resulting in, for example, distinctive American, British, French and Swiss hotel aesthetics and forms. Resort types responded to distinctive social as well as geographic considerations in places such as Australia, where Richard White (2012) argues that a distinctive culture produced a different resort culture and form than in England. There were often strong regional inflections in hotel development, reflected in design, geography of development, and other factors. The Florida winter resort, for example, was a species of hotel whose chronology of development, aesthetics and forms were different from grand urban hotels of the American north-east, mid-west and west coast, and reflected distinctive patterns of land and transport development, as well as climate and leisure patterns. Indeed, Florida's hotels have attracted considerable attention not just for their flamboyant form (see Figure 2.1, a postcard image of St. Augustine's Hotel Alcazar), but also for their integration within railway networks that were developed by key figures such as Henry Flagler (Braden, 2002; Graham, 2014; Revells, 2011). But, for the most part, according to the meta-narrative of the grand hotel's rise, these variations on a theme do not obscure an essential, stable institutional form: by the mid-19th century the grand hotel became a transnational category of Western commercial lodging denoting a luxurious institution adopting various national forms, servicing a cosmopolitan, capitalist elite. Nineteenth-century imperialism also brought European grand hotels to colonies and places where Western travellers toured and resorted in ever-greater numbers, from areas of formal political control in such places as French Indo-China, colonial Africa and South-East Asia, to places over which Western powers exercised political hegemony, such as Egypt, and those areas of settlement, such as Canada, which enjoyed a high degree of political and economic autonomy, but where hotel styles still proclaimed the influence of the European colonial project. As legible markers of colonial power, the hotel was often among the visible elements of the built environment.

This meta-narrative of the rise of the 19th-century grand hotel takes a critically important excursion into the non-colonial New World. The American hotel's colonial era would wait until the Spanish American War in 1898. In the meantime, within the borders of the new republic, historians have detected ways that the institution developed along a distinctive

Figure 2.1 The Alcazar, St. Augustine, Florida, ca. 1903–1904

path from the beginning of the 19th century, assuming a central role in the political life of the nation. Switzerland may have dominated the continental market in 'hotel science' by the late 19th century, and the capitals of Europe may have boasted a supposedly unrivalled culture of personal attendance, but, as we have seen in Chapter 1, scholars contend that their hotels also projected an ethos of patrician privilege and exclusivity that sustained and even strengthened traditional social stratifications and values within the hotel form. In contrast, American hotels, from an early stage, were fêted as incubators of a unique commercial ethos and civic disposition. As they assumed forms distinct from the resort complexes of the antebellum era (Chambers, 2001; Gassen, 2008; Sterngass, 2003), they wedded scientific management to technological innovation and became part of the fabric not only of a vibrant civic life, but also of dynamic local, regional and national networks.

There is evidence of America's precocious exceptionalism in its commercial hospitality sector wherever historians cast their eye, since contemporaries were often eager to record the singularity of the American hotel – and historians have generally reaffirmed their claims. Extensive and meticulous systematisation marked the American hotel, partly engendered by an imperative to find substitutes for scarce or expensive manual labour in the yeoman's republic. One observer wryly noted in a comparison of American and European hotels that the latter was adjudged to offer superior services: 'what we lack in ready hands and feet, we make up in labour-saving contrivances, so that the Modern American Hotel is a marvel of mechanical and labour-saving ingenuity, as well as a miracle of systematic order in the conduct of its daily life' (Modern Hotels, 1898: 487). What was it about the modern grand hotel that directs scholars of the modern hotel to find its epitome in America? Why did it elicit such extensive contemporary commentary on its uniqueness? To one 1873 observer, it was half-machine, half-creature – a gigantic 'living organism' under the command of the hotel-keeper. Its 'inner life' was an object of marvel – as complex and articulated as that of the nervous system:

> What is it? Physically speaking, a monster structure, many stories in height, covering numerous city lots, containing rooms by the hundred, and more or less capable of giving comfortable lodgment to many hundreds and perhaps a thousand guests; but, under a pressure like that of a Presidential convention, it can swallow up and stow away another equally numerous quota. It is a massive pile of marble, and brick, and slate, and iron, with a handsome architectural front, and so vermiculated, at stated and well-chosen intervals, with water-pipes and steam-pipes, gas-pipes and drain-pipes, speaking-tubes and nerve-like bell-wires, that, viewed as a whole, it is like a

living organism. It certainly constitutes a marvelous mechanical monument, to 'the whole glorious brotherhood of industrial inventors.'

In studying its inner life – that adaptation of means and organization of forces by which its vast aggregate of comfort and enjoyment is achieved, so that every reasonable physical want is supplied instantly and completely – we begin to see that it has a brain and a will, and we plainly perceive why *the man who can keep a hotel* has become the synonym for supreme and unimpeachable capacity. (Modern Hotels, 1873: 488)

If the *fin-de-siècle* American grand hotel seemed to boast awe-inspiring technological innovations, a vast and unrivalled scale, and a high level of efficient, internal organisation, across the Atlantic there was growing consternation at the size and impersonality of the modern hotel as an institution. In Britain such anxiety nurtured a distinctive strain of hotel history in the early 20th century. The British hotels' imperfections were laid bare, especially in relation to the American form, and these were grafted onto a wider malaise over waning economic power. This framework nourished a powerful, nostalgic interpretation of the English inn as a cultural form. Anxiety over its displacement found expression in a master-narrative that insisted that the limited liability hotel company risked extinguishing an authentic national institution. As the industrial age advanced and other countries claimed the mantle of innovation in a broad range of industrial and service sectors, eclipsing the mid-19th-century Workshop of the World, prolific amateur historians fetishised a particular construction of the English institution in narratives of 'bygone inns'. At the same time, American scholars surveyed and expounded on the characteristics of a purportedly indigenous form, acclaiming it as a signifier of a bold and new political experiment.

The Twentieth-Century Hotel

The narrative of progressive hotel innovation led by America in the 19th century, which centres on the hotel as a powerful expression of modernity, is consolidated in the historiography of the sector in the early 20th century. Scholarship charts the sector's continuing technologisation, coupled with a focus on managerial innovations associated with the republic (Mentzer, 2010). New hotels blurred old types. As elements of service and luxury once associated with the grand hotel were widely diffused (Davidson, 2005a), for example, the spatial regimes of hotels grew even more complex. These developments reflected the embeddedness of the hotel system within urban economies and their embrace of urban consumer culture, which they sought to reflect back onto the streets of their cities with even greater intensity (Knoch, 2008: 138–139, 140–143). The hotel incorporated retailers and services, from dress shops to barbers. Its lobby became a kind of thoroughfare and market: this extended the historical imbrication of the American hotel and the street, and a consolidation of the unique functions of the hotel's public spaces as a metaphorical public square.

The century also witnessed a number of developments that transformed commercial lodgings, with profound implications for their geographical distribution, functions, ownership and operation. In the late 19th century the bicycle, an underappreciated technology of locomotion that opened the field of travel to many people, impacted demand for commercial accommodation. The cycling tourist, for example, gave a fillip to the rural inn. But among the most transformative factors shaping new forms of accommodation and styles of travel was the development of the automobile, which gave rise to the American 'autocamp' and, later, the motel, and forwarded into a new age of mechanical locomotion an essential analytic link that has long been postulated between lodging networks and transport systems. The postwar motel, whose origins John A. Jakle *et al.* (1996) have traced to the western America autocamps, evolved into a series of accommodation structures distinguished by their design – cabin camps, then motor courts, the latter morphing into the modern motel in the postwar era. The motel boasted a distinctive architecture, integrating units under single roofs, with access from outside doors, stairs and balconies, minimal lobby space and often with restaurants attached. Motels multiplied as the freeway system expanded. They have become central to analyses of automobility and also of immigrant entrepreneurship, especially given the significant presence of Indo-Americans in the sector (Dhingra, 2012). Pawan Dhingra (2012: 11), for example, uses a case study of Ohio Indo-American hotel owners in the heart of the mythologised, but also increasingly economically challenged, 'Midwest' to explore, with the tools of critical race theory, patterns of 'differential inclusion' which have characterised the incorporation of immigrant and ethnic groups within the American neoliberal order. Lodgings here become a means of exploring a metaphorical dimension of mobility.

Hotel companies continued to identify, devise and pursue forms of revenue beyond the provision of accommodation and food, including conventions, weddings, partnerships with casinos and other strategies. At the same time, the locational advantages of central business district hotels in many major Western cities were in some, but not all, cases eroded by the evolution of new urban morphologies through: (1) suburbanisation; (2)

the development of nodes to service new transport infrastructures such as highways and airports; and (3) urban regeneration schemes. Within the context of changing urban forms, markets, technologies, travel preferences and transformations in the distribution and forms of commercial accommodation, the prestige value of some city-centre historic hotels remained strong, tapping a wellspring of nostalgia that hotels employed in programmatic heritage branding exercises. But translating a storied past into contemporary cachet was not guaranteed. Many historic grand hotels withered and 'died', some gracefully after a prolonged decline, some euthanised by the wrecking ball – many generating sentimental chronicles of their fame, fading glory and demise.

It is tempting to see this era as a decisive moment in hotel history, especially in America, where many of these innovations were realised. Yet Lisa Pfueller Davidson (2005a: 100) contends that the emergence of the motel, changes in location preferences for travellers and transformations in mobility and travel practices must be interpreted through the long lens of institutional evolution as a way in which the American system of commercial accommodation nimbly adapted to market demand. In this sense, it was a continuation of its historical culture of efficiency and structural mutability. In the first decades of the 20th century, Davidson contends that the commercial hotel began to adopt elements of service culture previously associated with the grand hotel, and also became more functionally and spatially complex. There were other innovations, too, that harnessed the signifiers of 'traditional' institutions, including their names and forms, and incorporated them within 20th-century lodgings. As the automobile was adopted as a principal means of locomotion from the interwar-period, for example, some new establishments in England adopted the 'old inn' moniker (and some elements of its aesthetic), partly as a response to the retrospective valorisation of an imagined space of intimacy and conviviality engendered by a wave of inn-nostalgia (Bates, 2003).

If limited liability had once supplied a principle for hotel development on an expanded scale in the 19th century, new structures of capital investment, ownership and management emerged in the 20th century that underpinned the sector's growth. Regional, national and global expansion through forms of corporate organisation, such as the chain system, which had long been present in Europe but found its more experimental form in America, and business innovations that included separation of ownership, franchising and property management roles, reflected the priorities of multinational corporations and strategies to mitigate risk in building an ever-more profitable brand. Indeed, the proliferation of brands in the post-World War II era, even within a single lodging category such as the motel, heralded processes of corporate consolidation, product differentiation and market segmentation which often left late 20th-century travellers posing the existential question 'where am I?' when they passed through the entrance of a franchised hotel, sometimes architecturally indistinct from others that were thousands of miles away. All the while, the new American hotel, wherever in the world it was found, continued to signify the epitome of modernity and comfort, and also the political, cultural and economic power of that country, as old grand hotels followed divergent paths of revitalisation and decline.

Hotel Spaces and Social Codes: Liminality, Permissiveness and Transgression

The narrative of the modern hotel that is sketched above plots the emergence of distinctive forms of commercial accommodation linked to the organisation of capital, transport and mobility systems, and political and commercial networks. The three topics covered by this book have offered fertile ground for scholars to test its claims. Of all the manifestations of the modern hotel, the grand hotel exercises the strongest hold over popular imagination, in part because of its prominence in film and literature. The European grand hotel conjures not only an image of a large-scale, externally ornate edifice with sumptuous interiors, but also a culture of service – lavish, attentive and professional – and an aura of mannered exclusiveness marked by elaborate rituals and a culture of elite, cosmopolitan patronage that seems to affirm the proposition that it has internalised and propagated the ethos of the private country house. But, of course, the archetypal grand hotel, despite a presence that has loomed as large over the popular imagination as the grandest and most ostentatious establishments did over city blocks, always constituted a comparatively low proportion of hostelries. A 'hotel' in the 19th and 20th centuries, as now, denoted a markedly diverse set of institutional types, united in their provision of commercial accommodation, but often on very different terms, to a range of markets, and within markedly different building types – some which bore the name were little more than lowly rural outposts which, like the Mena, Arkansas establishment illustrated in Figure 2.2, combined hotel, post-office, public-house and other functions (MacLaren *et al.*, 2011). By the 20th century, the term subsumed such a wide range of establishments that writers such as Norman S. Hayner found it necessary to delineate a typology and provide an operating definition for his own use. Hayner decried the looseness of a nomenclature that

Calvin Photographic Collection -- The University of Iowa Paleontology Repository

Figure 2.2 Big Fork Hotel and Post Office, Mena, Arkansas, late 1890s or early 1900s

encompassed steamships, railway cars and clubs (1936: 47). Indeed, many observers defined the hotel primarily in relational terms, and especially through comparison to the home. To some sociologists interpreting the patterning of class relations in the grand hotel, its historical institutionalisation of the ethos of the aristocratic abode is a critical concern. To other scholars, the hotel supplied an 'escape' from mundane domestic space – as well as opportunities to contest and reconstruct normative values and social relations that prevailed outside its walls.

By the late 19th century, a growing number of people, especially in America, inhabited the hotel on a permanent basis. This practice casts debates about the hotel and the home as distinct institutions in sharp relief. The choice of the hotel as a permanent abode drew extensive commentary (and no small degree of disquiet). This new category of permanent hotel resident challenged prevailing ideas of the hotel as a temporary place of accommodation – as a place that was defined in contrast to the home and prevailing ideals of domesticity. Historically, hotels generated anxiety and considerable commentary when they seemed to licence, structure and sustain codes of racial, gender and class interaction that were forbidden outside its confines. Commentators then treated the hotel as a potential incubator of pathology. In the 1930s, the American sociologist Norman S. Hayner (1928: 784) identified the susceptibility of hotel dwellers, even those who were of respectable standing in their communities, to slide into a 'moral holiday' and forsake codes of conduct which otherwise forbade theft and other violations. It offered an alternative to the structured, normative domesticity that was acted out in homes and neighbourhoods. Even when the hotel detective, hotel staff and elaborate processes of registration were enlisted to define and police hotel behaviours, the nature of hotel space, and its status as an institution open to the public, facilitated transgressive behaviours.

Recent studies seek to analyse hotel spaces and behaviours without adjudging their morality, but instead asking whether or not they are institutionalised not only within hotel culture and enabled by hotel design. Concepts such as liminality and alterity have been applied to shed light on the slipperiness of social norms amid blurred public and private spaces and to explore the hotel as a space conducive to the subversion of social and cultural codes (Pritchard & Morgan, 2006). Scholars suggest a high level of constructedness to hotels' 'permissiveness'. Caroline Field Levander and Matthew Pratt Guterl (2015) note, for example, the ambiguities telegraphed by the modern hotel in relation to sexuality: the hotel room itself is an architecture of permissiveness, creatively producing a platform for sexual encounters. Scholars have explored a number of historical examples of commercial accommodation in which licence for particular 'illicit' behaviours are signalled by the location of the hotel within urban spaces, and facilitated by its internal spatial logic. They have found modern exemplars in Asia. There, the post-World War II Japanese and Taiwanese love hotel emerged in response to particular socio-economic and cultural circumstances that inhibited sexual activity in homes by supplying institutions which enabled sexual encounters (Chaplin, 2007; Chang et al., 2012). Hotels offered the affordances for sexual identities to be reconstituted in putatively private space (Pritchard & Morgan, 2006: 767). Behaviour that was proscribed in the home, owing to cultural taboos or constraints of space that inhibited privacy, was normalised within the rooms of the hotel. The locations of the Japanese love hotels, in laneways often close to railway lines, reinforced a conflation of illicit sexual activities with the marginal spaces of the city they inhabited, and also demarcated them from 'neighbourhoods' (Chaplin, 2007: 184). But if the exterior spaces, including discrete entranceways, signified secretiveness, the interior spaces, both public (the lobby, where discretion reigned) and, more dramatically, the fantasy realm of the bedroom, authorised and ordered sexual interactions in explicit ways. Broadly similar arguments may be made regarding many Niagara Falls hotels, where sexual adventure was often explicitly underscored as part of the attraction (Dubinsky, 1999).

Barbara Penner (2004) has dissected the Honeymoon suite in hotels in the postwar Pocono Mountains, in northwest Pennsylvania. She identifies them as sites in which lavish design, props, mirrors, and commercial promotion cultivated a hedonistic imagination, as its affordances shaped choreographies of movement within the rooms. Other scholars examine how the historical development and evolution of hotels and motels organised around homosexual sociabilities and other gendered identities and performances were influenced by legal and cultural regimes which variously authorised or proscribed public identification of a homosexual market, and the public operation of establishments that catered to it. Such establishments have ranged from sites of furtive behaviour in known networks of clandestine establishments to those which explicitly targeted a homosexual market segment (Auer, 2013; Branchik, 2002; Cook, 2003: 27–28; Krahulik, 2005). The resorts of Provincetown, Massachusetts, for example, were historically established as (still heavily gendered) 'queer spaces' (Krahulik, 2005) even as homosexual activity was outlawed through the United States of America. Scholars of sexuality and the hotel who are developing new perspectives on homosexual identities, businesses and market segments have not sought to explicate the potentialities for 'deviance' that inheres in the modern hotel form, as Norman S. Hayner did, as much as they seek to understand how ideas of normative and aberrant behaviours were historically coded within the spaces of commercial accommodation. In some hotels and resorts, dominant social codes reconstructed those that prevailed outside the hotel's walls and inverted those of the home.

The possibilities of code- and convention-reconstruction are expressions of the ambiguous space that the hotel has historically occupied between public and private, between home and away. To some extent, the hotel and home depended on each other, and the affordances and codes that the other space supplied and activated. A.K. Sandoval-Strausz (2007: 203) theorises the idea of the hotel as a site of transgression by underscoring hotels' position as 'open establishments': illicit assignations were historically enabled by the affordances of transient residence, and theft was facilitated by the public nature of many hotel spaces, which admitted people from the street into the hotel. He argues that efforts to surveille and regulate these activities constituted ways in which the institutions navigated modernity (Sandoval-Strausz, 2007: 221). Hotels, such as New York's Chelsea Hotel (Figure 2.3), could function as a metaphorical shelter from the dominant culture in other ways, incubating profoundly influential, often counter-cultural, artistic movements (Fick, 2017; Miles, 2001).

Figure 2.3 Chelsea Hotel, 222 West 23rd Street, Manhattan, 1936

It is instructive to incorporate hotel employees within the framework of studying thresholds, liminality, boundaries and behaviours in the context of hotels, such as adultery and theft, and also useful for exploring their participation in the hotel's spaces of 'escape' from the strictures of the home (James, 2012; Sandoval-Strausz, 2007: 203–227). Roy C. Wood (1992) has explored, in contemporary analyses, the hotel workforce as 'marginal' – nomadic in character, and prone to unconventional moral and social behaviours. While A.K. Sandoval-Strausz (2007) offers an analysis of the historical workforce which contends that they functioned as key agents of surveillance within hotels, Wood suggests that hotel employees can been seen as operating within a culture with affordances for behaviours such as purloining of goods and sexual transgression. Wood argues that the treatment of such workers as 'predisposed towards deviant behaviour' fails to account for the 'opportunity structure' of employment enabling such behaviour – not least through the licence granted to guests and the normalisation of their transgressive behaviour. Forms of sociability specific to such 'hotel life' are exemplified by sociological studies in the pre-World War II period. One enumerated hotel slang words in an effort to capture the dynamics of communication among hotel workers that were impenetrable to the guest (Cornyn, 1939). The sheer number of terms that reference sex – 'broad', 'dish', 'gash', 'girl' and 'hooker' all denoting a prostitute, for example (Cornyn 1939) – suggests the extent of staff surveillance over, and knowledge of, guests' 'private' behaviours. But the lexicon also reveals a growing fissure between staff and guests that characterised the large, differentiated workforce of the grand hotel, exemplified by coteries of workers segregated by skill, gender, age, race and ethnicity (see Figure 2.4, depicting the large, male kitchen staff at Brown Hotel in Louisville, Kentucky in 1939). Historically, at particular moments in particular places, the behaviour of both guests and employees was a focus of concern: the heavy surveillance placed over both during wartime, and especially the expulsion of those employees who were nationals of a belligerent state – Germans, for example, in Allied states during the World Wars – points to fruitful ways in which processes of 'becoming' deviant are contingent upon social, cultural and political contexts, and how structures of surveillance were shaped and reshaped over time. Indeed, 'home' can denote not only

Figure 2.4 Kitchen staff, Brown Hotel, Louisville, Kentucky, 1929

the intimate domestic realm but also, in cases revealed by the expulsion of hotel labour, a 'home country' outside which its nationals can exploit the subversive potentials of the hotel.

Hotel Types and Cultures

Many studies explore the large-scale hotel, with its scale, anonymity and complex spatial regimes, as a place of subversive and creative potential. The size and profile of labour forces and markets, as well as locations and business structures, vary greatly by institution. Hotels have assumed an immense range of forms, and it is valuable to briefly explore some of the critical axes along which hotels and hotel types diverge. As A.K. Sandoval-Strausz (2007) notes in his survey of American hotel history, the expansion of accommodation types in the 19th century requires clarifications of their different forms, purposes and clienteles. To this end, he proposes seven key types (81–99): luxury hotels, commercial hotels, middle-class hotels, marginal hotels, resorts, railroad hotels and settlement hotels. Similarly, Martina Krebs (2009: 21) has proposed a useful scheme for categorising present-day institutions. We might similarly conceive of hotels inhabiting a continuum. While not entirely distinctive categories, specific features and functions historically differentiated many of the core types, running from grand/palace hotels and high-end resort hotels on one end, through commercial and family hotels, to rudimentary hostels servicing a particular market segment, to downtown rooming houses which adopted the hotel appellation at the other end. Several criteria depicted in Figure 2.5 underpin the relational typology (which excludes non-commercial establishments that do not charge a fee or require some compensation in return for temporary lodging, and also excludes institutions which have emerged in the past few decades and constitute what Rob MacDonald (2000) has described as 'new *hybrid* urban hotels' (italics in original quotation)).

These characteristics underlay 19th- and 20th-century travellers', guidebook writers' and other commentators' evaluations of establishments. Small towns, villages and rural areas boasted buildings that proclaimed themselves to be 'hotels' – but travellers knew to expect a different building type, as well as standards of service, systems of labour, range of amenities and charges than in fashionable hotel districts of major metropolitan areas. However, contemporaries were also attuned to the strategic adoption of names to disguise an essentially different institutional *type*, especially when modest establishments claimed the mantle and the

Characteristic	Elaboration
Services and Amenities	Level of service and quality of amenities and ancillary services, sometimes externally evaluated according to 'star' rankings
Location	Central or marginal location – this can change over time
Scale	Size of the establishment
Labour and Management Structure	Size of the workforce, and the organisation and hierarchies of labour, as well as the participation of a manager and a manager's family in operations
Scale and Organisation of Capital	Scale, organisation and levels of capital used to realise and operate an establishment
Specialised Institutional Function(s)	Whether the establishment is associated with specific functions – leisure, commerce, or health-related practices, and whether the provision of room and/or board are combined with other services and functions
Clientele(s)	The market; a variety of intersecting axes may be relevant, including socio-economic status, gender, race, ethnicity and age, as well as a geographic market area
Original Form(s) and Adaptation(s)	Degree to which the structure is purpose-built or partly or wholly adapted to the purposes of commercial accommodation
Internal Organisation	Levels of internal spatial complexity, including extent of space that is dedicated to, or can be repurposed for non-lodging activities such as events, retail outlets and services
Provision of Fare	Provision of fare or premises to partake of food on-site, the variety and formality of such premises and the type(s) of food and beverage(s) available
Costs	Cost to users of various goods and services
Social Tone/Prestige Value	Often intangible, the reputational or prestige value, as well as the 'atmosphere', of an establishment – its 'social tone'

Figure 2.5 Criteria for a hotel typology

pretensions of the hotel. They often met with mockery and withering disdain, the distinction between a lofty title and the building it signified providing scope for both humour and cultural critique which suggested that they were evaluated as belonging to another category of accommodation (James, 2012).

In interrogating what constituted the identity of a hotel, exploring the intangible qualities that created hotel life, and producing a hierarchy of types, 'hotel culture' is a valuable but elusive organising concept, denoting a range of affective dispositions cultivated and expressed towards particular establishments and categories of accommodation. They involve enactments within hotels that reflect how a hotel's meaning is crafted, projected and consumed, consciously and unconsciously, by many actors. Hotels offer spaces for the performance of collective 'belonging', and they inculcate specific practices through the organisation of space, their aesthetics and the cultural capital which Michael Riley (1984) has identified as a critical regulator of class participation in hotel culture. Hotel culture conceptualises these intangible webs of meaning. The choice of a hotel by guests, and by staff as a place of employment, constitutes enlistment in, and participation in reproducing, its culture. Frustratingly, but perhaps necessarily, vague, hotel culture can explain how people experience hotels, and how institutional identities are cultivated and curated, produced and reproduced. Hotel culture anchors the hierarchy of types in Figure 2.6.

Atop the hierarchy, where exclusivity was expressed in high charges, opulent ornamentation and extravagant comforts, stood the grand hotel – with its large and highly differentiated labour force, its affluent guests, its technologised services, its premier, central location, its lavish interior and exterior appointment, its restaurants offering high-status (often 'foreign', especially French) fare, and its complex internal spatial regimes. These features, as Molly Berger (2011: 22–23) notes, were associated with the 'first-class' American hotel from its emergence in the 19th century. The luxury resort, which was an institution primarily defined by leisure uses and was often characterised by the attractions of climate, water and other features associated with the restoration or maintenance of health, frequently boasted a grand hotel, though resorts

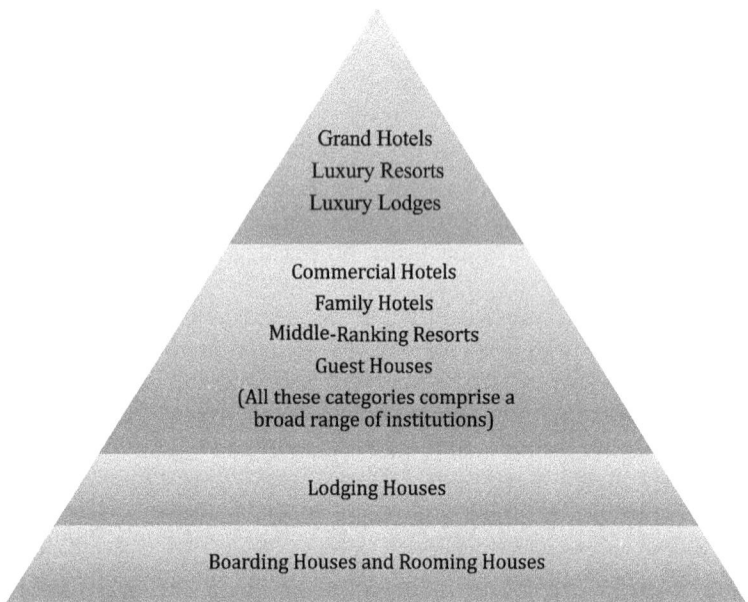

Figure 2.6 A hierarchy of hotel culture

of different ranks, serving different markets, appeared throughout the continuum, from the most exclusive national and international institutions to the much more modest local and regional resorts. Moving down the hierarchy there is a very broad tier boasting many hotel types, all defined by a less exclusive culture than the grand hotel and resort, and by a diversity of amenities. The commercial hotel, at least in the 19th century, was less exclusive. Many, but not all, were built on a smaller scale than the grand hotel. It took the form of a generally less ornate edifice and was geared towards a broader and more mixed constituency, often catering to commercial figures (French, 2010, 2005). It boasted considerably more modest appointments and services. Often strategically situated in commercial centres with high levels of mobility (Hayner, 1936: 28), it was frequently owned by an individual, family, partnership, or small-scale limited liability concern. In some places, a commercial hotel advertised itself as a 'Family Hotel', or, reflecting currents of the day, tailored its hospitality to the precepts of 'Temperance' (such 'respectable' principles, however, were difficult to maintain in a competitive market where the extent of demand was limited). The mid-point of the hierarchy encompasses a range of such types – including 'guest houses' at the lower end, especially for accommodation in seaside and other resorts. At the bottom of the hierarchy are lodging houses – distinguished, according by Norman S. Hayner, from rooming houses 'by the payment of weekly rather than monthly rent, by the prevalence of mixed clienteles in the rooming house, and by inferior location, in marginal or deteriorating areas' (Hayner, 1936: 28–29). For many social investigators and commentators, they were a focus of particular concern, owing to their overlapping spaces and difficulty to fix on a social register (given its mixture of residents (Crook, 2008)). They offered rudimentary accommodation, and were often operated by individuals. Their inhabitants were drawn from sections of the population whose socio-economic marginality was matched by the physical location of the establishments themselves. Although they are not the subject of this book, the boarding house and the rooming house have generated important scholarship (Gamber, 2007; Groth, 1994; Jakle et al., 1996) that has expanded our understanding of the variety of commercial hostelries, their functions and markets (notably in America and in places such as Blackpool (Walton, 1978)), emphasised their critical role in urban economies, and explored the ways in which they were durably lodged in popular consciousness. In seeking to chart the histories of one or a group of these establishments, historians have tended to adopt distinctive approaches, each with its own epistemological frame.

Methods and Narratives in Hotel History

Until fairly recently, scholarship on the hotel as an historical institution was not weighty enough to develop a sustained historiographical survey. In 1991 Robert H. Woods (1991), in a survey of relevant US literature, noted the paucity of such scholarship. He identified a literature that he broadly categorised as: (1) biographical (according agency in the sector's development to an innovative business figure); (2) company histories (which tended towards descriptive, rather than analytic, narratives); and (3) teaching case studies (which focused on a particular business 'problem' and decisions surrounding it). Although popular histories were numerous, critical scholarship was highly limited to a few studies, such as Warren James Belasco's (1979) study of the autocamp and motel, which largely treated the accommodation sector as a subsidiary focus, with its primary interest in the car – a 20th-century corollary to the tight heuristic linkages between innovations in transport technologies and accommodation types (Woods, 1991: 92). Burgeoning interest in the hotel over the past two decades has made a more updated survey of this historical scholarship both possible and necessary. The hotel interests scholars in the applied hotel and hospitality sector, and critical tourism scholars, too. To historians, until the past few decades, the hotel seems to have been largely dismissed as little more than what Alasdair Pettinger (2013) describes as a 'transit zone', rather than a site of meaningful activity. As interest in the identity and meaning of the hotel has expanded, they have embraced the insights and methods of sociology and other disciplines. Contemporary critical scholarship, in contrast to earlier sociologies of the modern hotel, argues that it was not so much a *manifestation* of grand processes of modernisation as a *shaper* and *signifier* of social, cultural, commercial and political development. More than a conduit, the hotel gave form to social, cultural, economic and political relations, and was an actor in its own right (Fick, 2017). Hotels projected, moulded and carried ideologies, rather than only instantiating them. In undertaking critical hotel history that advances this argument, scholars have adopted a variety of approaches.

Design and Construction Perspectives

Critical scholarship has focused on interrogating processes of imagining and realising hotels that involve histories of technology, design and construction, and the political and cultural environments in which hotels were envisioned and erected. This approach reflects the strong influence of art and architectural history, the history of science and technology, and the spatial turn in the social sciences. Some enquiries, many focusing on American hotels, take as their structuring principle the professional biographies of particular architects, such as Lawrence Murray Dixon (Lejeune & Shulman, 2000), or architectural partnerships, such as Chicago's Holabird and Roche (Bruegmann, 1997) and the American firm of Schultze and Weaver, which produced such landmark buildings as the Waldorf-Astoria (Dolkart, 2005; Lamonaca & Mogul, 2005). Although these studies often explore buildings in a number of places, sometimes a particular architect or firm is seen as intimately linked to, and studied as a catalyst for, the development of a particular locality's hotel topography. Their impact is seen as decisive in shaping the identity of the building, and often the broader urban environment. Let us take the example of one of America's most eminent, and studied, post-World War II hotel architects, Morris Lapidus. Lapidus is regarded as exerting tremendous influence, through hotel design, over the whimsical aesthetics of Miami Beach, his hotels signifying a particular form of glamour. Lapidus's buildings were strongly associated with one particular era and area, and its distinctive economy and culture. Hotels such as the Fontainebleau (Figure 2.7) instantiated design innovation, but they are seen, beyond meriting attention on those grounds, as iconic shapers and signifiers of a peculiarly American postwar form of leisure and modernity. Some studies of Morris Lapidus's critically derided but profoundly influential Miami Beach hotels have emphasised performances that were shaped by affordances such as the hotel staircase (Friedman, 2005; Philippou, 2013). The Fontainebleau's iconic lobby stairs (Figure 2.8), for example, shaped an elaborate choreography through opulent space. George E. Thomas and Susan Nigra Snyder (2005: 208) interpret Lapidus's designs as developing within the dominant, suburban, mode of postwar life, taking the suburban ideal and, in the Fontainebleau and Eden Roc Hotels, producing a kaleidoscopic 'dream escape'.

Through these distinctive forms, Lapidus, the developers who financed the hotels and the hotels' owners, translated Miami Beach to the wider world as a site of hedonism and glamour (Friedman, 2005) in fantasy-scapes that produced a Miami hotel form recognisable around the world. Alice T. Friedman (2005: 219–220, 232–233) likens Lapidus's adaptation of Art Deco forms to the visual evocation of ocean liners, mimicking the amenities and interior opulence of those externally more austere vessels as he adopted the hotel as the primary medium for his architectural imagination. This focus came after several decades focused on other buildings, including commercial commissions which later exerted profound influence over Lapidus's treatment of the hotel as a site of lavish consumption and performance (Friedman, 2005). The Catskills, long a centre of

Figure 2.7 Fontainebleau Hotel, Miami Beach, Florida, 1955

(especially Jewish) tourist patronage, could not compete with the extravagance and inventiveness that was making Miami Beach a magnet for tourists and travellers. As Lapidus's buildings attest, hotel aesthetics, both interior and exterior, reveal broader shifts in taste, available materials and technologies and changing ideas about the relationship between form and function, and how they influence hotel styles (Davidson, 2005a). They show also how hotels can exert power over their wider urban environment – to the point where they can define it. Design has imaginative components, but in most studies hotel design is grounded in analyses of technologies of production and materials of construction. Construction is therefore a major concern of design history, highlighting important elements of analysis that risk being elided by focusing principally on exterior and interior aesthetics. Construction history as a separate field tends to focus on novel techniques, the innovative use of materials, or the use of new materials such as steel frames (e.g. Jackson, 1998), and can reveal interwoven economic and ideological incentives.

By marrying a study of the design and construction history of hotels with readings of the buildings as artefacts of relations of political and

Figure 2.8 Fontainebleau Hotel, Miami Beach, Florida. General view of lobby, 1955

cultural power, scholars have charted the ways in which urban hotelscapes materialise cultural and political relations as well as technological developments. Annabel Wharton (2001) ably adopts this stance in her analysis of Hilton Hotels. Her study interweaves personal and building biographies to explore the interlacing of Cold War ideologies, Conrad Hilton's personal politics and the business strategies of Hilton International and other actors as they participated in the erection of hotels after World War II. Projects of hotel financing and construction implicated a host of organisations and people with a range of priorities and incentives, from the State Department, to local sources of finance in the countries where hotels were erected. From this matrix of relationships emerged a distinctive programme with its own logic that married the priorities of these actors. Locational choice and building design, including exterior aesthetics and internal spatial organisation, crystallised strategies for projecting American power and ideologies. Hilton hotels, from Athens, to Berlin, to Cairo, served as vectors for aesthetic and consumerist ideals that were linked to the postwar hegemon's political and economic power and cultural clout. Wharton's innovative hotel history underscores the potent political, economic and cultural symbolisms that attach to the American hotel as an institution – and how they are inscribed in diverse spaces. She also underscores a critical point elaborated by scholars of the colonial and postcolonial hotel: the materialities of the hotel, especially its windows, terraces and verandas, 'frame' space and structure gazes inward and outward in freighted ways. The spaces that hotels inhabit, the landscapes of which they were a part, and which they produce through their vantage-points, are critical concerns. But Wharton, like others, is also interested in what happens *within* hotel spaces, partly as a function of their design, but also as relations of gender, race and socio-economic authority are played out within their myriad spaces.

Construction and design histories can, then, be organised around, or incorporate, the study of particular interior spatialities across a number of hotels (Avermaete & Massey, 2013; Brucken, 1996; Penner, 2010; Wharton, 2001). This approach allows scholars to explore ways in which technologies, evolving social and cultural codes and behaviours, consumer regimes and ideas about public and private space were conceptualised, realised, performed and contested within the networked spaces of hotels: the lobby, the lounge, the front desk, the elevator, the sample room and café. Sometimes they focus on one such place.

Deconstructing Interior Spatial Regimes and Sociabilities

The hotel lobby, such as that of Boston's Hotel Touraine (Figure 2.9), has performed a starring role in accounts of hotel spaces, from the grand hotel novel and film to the motel horror flick (Avermaete & Massey, 2013; Berens, 1997; Clarke *et al.*, 2009; Matthias, 2006; Tallack, 2002; Wharton, 2007). It has been a site of thorough historical analysis, often from a dramaturgical perspective, with Carol Berens (1997) seeing it (and the hotel bar) as a 'scripted' site eliciting particular affective responses and behaviours. People pass through doors, 'peacock alleys' and 'grand staircases' as actors and spectators/*flâneurs*, participating in dramas structured by the affordances of these spaces (Berens, 1997: 2, 23). Scholars of the hotel lobby have dissected the interplay between its physical layout, its décor and its ambiguous status as space that is neither public nor private. It plays a critical role in hotel systems and performances of surveillance, management and technology, and shapes cultures of sociability. Indeed, scholars of sociology, literature and film have evinced an abiding interest in this particular space – and historians have seized on its importance, too.

Donald McNeill (2008: 384), noting that hotels comprise many highly private spaces, has underscored that the lobby serves a number of

Figure 2.9 Grand staircase and lobby, Hotel Touraine, Boston, Mass, ca. 1908–1909

important symbolic and material functions: as a site of often highly decorative interior aesthetics, and a place where social interactions are performed. Norman S. Hayner (1936: 144) regarded the American lobby as a
species of 'public square' and saw a paradoxical social regime prevailing
in a place that rendered the subject both free and profoundly lonely
(Hayner, 1928: 789–790). Theorist Siegfried Kracauer (2004), writing in
the Weimar era, contended that the hotel lobby was the apotheosis of a
peculiarly modern form of alienation and anomie. Kracauer, exploring the
character of the city and everyday practices through the prism of the
hotel's topography and social regimes (Katz, 1999: 135), likened the hotel
lobby to a 'negative church'. The individual was deprived of authentic
social communion; anonymity was no prerequisite for sociality. 'Trivial
conversation' was the obverse of prayer; silence found no transcendent
purpose, and the equality of the atomised figures of the lobby expressed
only their similar status vis-à-vis 'the nothing'. This was a despairing
appraisal, identifying the hotel as a primary object of theoretical concern
and the social relations it engendered as signifiers of the modern
condition.

As Marc Katz (1999: 140) contends in his analysis of the historical
context that gave rise to Kracauer's hotel lobby, the space upon which the
Weimar-era intellectual meditated was also becoming rationalised and

technologised, with a precision that contemporaries likened to machines. New imperatives emerged with respect to sanitising and surveilling the hotel lobby, and a large information gathering and monitoring apparatus was enlisted to this end, from the 'room-board' to the staff detective. These are concerns of modern historical scholarship, too, especially in relation to America's highly technologised palace hotels. The lobby rewards close analysis as part of the spatial-social complex of the hotel, part of the organisation of the hotel's interior spaces that pattern consumption. In examining the 'architectonics' of the hotel lobby, Tom Avermaete and Anne Massey (2013), for example, explore it as a site of Western modernity, combining both public and private elements and providing potentialities for negotiation between them. Its spaces order the syntax of social relations. The lobby and lounge are integral to the spatial systems of the hotel, but they are functionally and often aesthetically distinct. They influence choreographies associated with specific technologies (such as access and egress through the revolving door), registration at the reception desk, which functions as a centre controlling passage to the spaces beyond it, and movement into, within and out of stairs, escalators, elevators and other paths and technologies of mobility (Avermaete, 2013). The lobby's sociabilities and spaces were always inextricably connected – in all commercial hostelries, on all scales. But the modern hotel has seemed, if not to synchronise, then to align, them in new ways, according to a new logic, in the three theatres explored in this book. In America, it seemed, the hotel lobby also assumed particular civic importance, supplying space for intermingling, for coordination, and for a level of permeation and imbrication that made it a natural transition between the street and private spaces.

Building Biographies

One common approach to hotel history trains its sights on an establishment or group of establishments, adopting a historical *building biography* form – a longitudinal study thick in description that captures many dimensions of one hotel or several establishments' histories (e.g. Fick, 2017). It can chart interlaced histories of the buildings and forms of dwelling with them (McNeill & McNamara, 2009, 2012), focusing on iconic institutions – the Waldorf-Astoria in New York, or Raffles in Singapore – or comparatively less well-known establishments, emploting their experiences over time. It can focus on the relationship between the particular built form of the hotel and the functions it promotes, including the way it inhabits and constructs nature (Rosenbaum, 2016), shaped ideologies of health and fortification of the body (Jennings, 2003, 2007), or was enlisted in colonial and postcolonial politics and projects (Henderson, 2001). The individual building history or building 'prosopography' can also illuminate how hotel locations and forms express geopolitical currents. Vladimir Kulić (2014), for example, through the prism of a biography of the Babylon Hotel in Baghdad, weaves together the history of 'Mesopotamianism' – a movement to claim an independent Iraqi identity in the post- World War II era – with a narrative of the country's deep engagements in wider global networks. Indeed, its form manifested the influence of its Slovenian architect, and Iraq's affiliations with Yugoslavia. The hotel's design, therefore, reflected a *mélange* of influences, political incentives and ideological enlistments. Its realisation was testament to an infrastructure programme embedded within the global Non-Aligned movement, and also to globalised processes, as Baghdad assumed an increasingly important place on the world stage as an oil capital in the 1970s and 1980s. As an example of this complex transnational matrix, the management of the hotel was contracted to the same Indian company that owned the historic Mena House Hotel in Egypt. Kulić's building biography offers a striking way of bringing together social, economic, political, cultural, architectural, design and construction history in an analysis of one particular building. It often adopts an organic metaphor for the life-cycle of a building which links it to much broader narratives implicating the built and natural environment. It suggests how networks of capital and circulation involved in the life of the hotel can articulate links to broader networks outside its walls, and also outside the borders of the city, region and country in which it stands.

Analysing shifting and diverse affective dispositions towards hotels enables the study of how particular establishments become sites of potentially enormous (and contested) emotional investment through 'accumulated sentimental capital' as they evolve over time (McNeill & McNamara, 2012: 150). That capital was sometimes accrued through deliberate heritage programmes which reframed the establishments at least partially as 'tourist sites' in their own right (Henderson, 2004), and sometimes through the demolition of hotels and their re-materialisation in narratives constructed from memory and surviving objects – postcards and other ephemera – that served as the raw materials for vivid reimaginings. Indeed, dissecting the formation of narratives of demolition as part of critical building biographies can reveal deep and divided investments with which a variety of actors contended. Owners and developers, for example, may have negotiated resistance by proposing the 'necessity' of deliberate physical demolition, often invoking the imperatives of modernisation

(Jim, 2005). A powerful organic metaphor often underpins many building biographies, and moments of building 'death', can lay bare ideologies of technology and progress and reveal complex responses which demonstrate ways they functioned as monuments and repositories of collective memory and as sites of deep sentimental attachment. As Donald McNeill and Kim McNamara (2012: 158) observe, a 'demolition' narrative also starkly reveals the layered nature of 'place attachments, and how collective memory is distributed across attachments to *site*, to *building* and to *institution*'. Demolition reconfigures the materialities of the hotel, endowing physical fragments of its former form with meanings, and also produces narratives of place that reflect the diversity of a hotel's constituencies, from former employees to former guests. This agenda offers critical tools with which to examine the organic metaphor which undergirds many hotel histories, and also to understand the hotel as a *lieu de mémoire*.

As Karl Raitz and John Paul Jones (1998: 17) have argued, the study of urban geographies has tended to privilege the analysis of wider built environments, focusing little on individual sites. The analysis of built structures is liable to focus on rural 'folk types'. McNeill and McNamara (2012: 150–151), in sketching an agenda for the study of hotel biography, suggest an agenda for hotels to redress this imbalance. The 'cultural economy of buildings as systems', as well as the shifting building ontology – the construction of the meaning of narrative of a building – allows us to extend the analysis beyond the commemorative and heritage vein of hotel history, by questioning the ontology of the hotel. Demolition, for example, can reconfigure and strengthen some imaginative hotel identities as the hotel is dematerialised – even if the act of destruction creates the potential new projects which reignite the life cycle (Jim, 2005). Tracing the experience of hotels over time can do much to underscore their adaptive functions – when, for example, they are appropriated, sometimes coercively, for new purposes. Robert A. Davidson (2006), for example, has explored the social and cultural life and commercial functions of hotels in Catalonia, seeing them as sites of transculturation through which people, goods and cultural styles were received, adapted and circulated. European modernism found a vernacular expression in the late 19th-century Hotel Internacional, while in the interwar period Barcelona's vibrant hotel scene became a platform for a jazz culture that offered a stage for the elaboration of a critical interwar popular cultural movement. Instead of seeing the transformation of the hotel's functions in war as representing a break from these essential transcultural processes, though, Davidson argues that they are an extension of those roles. They are starkly illustrated by the study of hotels in a stateless nation whose centres of gravity were variously within and outside the Spanish state. The 'grand hotel's' conquest during the 1936–39 Spanish Civil War, and in the context of the international socialist and anarcho-syndicalist struggle for control of the city, demonstrates not only the strategic and symbolic significance of the site, but also the Catalan hotel's role mediating local political strife and the wider global movements of which it was a part (Davidson, 2006: 178–179). The changes in a hotel's identity, as Davidson shows, can be affected by means other than physical destruction.

As we shall see in Chapter 4, scholars studying Raffles Hotel in Singapore have underscored how the politics of its 'restoration' reveal the freighted decisions about how to 'preserve' the hotel – with the selection of 'representative' spaces and times periods revealing the strategies of the postcolonial state and businesses. Employing a longitudinal frame to analyse a specific site through building biography can incorporate the study of the meaning of place to these diverse groups, illuminate its shifting material qualities and symbolic values and condense the analysis of complex processes of 'memory making'. It weds design and construction history with the study of economic, social and cultural relations centred on the hotel, links the hotel's spaces to those that it inhabits, and incorporates the study of emotion and space which make it the subject of evolving stories. It can chart physical construction and destruction, but also imaginative reconstitution and meaning-making. In short, it can be employed to understand not only the 'life' of a hotel, as the commemorative approach has done, but also how that life is understood and contested over time.

Business and Economic Histories

While this interest in processes of place-making is heavily influenced by cultural history, there have been long-standing interests in the hotel among economic historians. One approach has placed heavy emphasis on individual captains of industry who steward the sector and particular establishments, and adopts a biographical or prosopographical form. Scholars examining how a 'hotel vision' was enacted not only by architects in their design of buildings and the articulation of its interior spatial regimes, but also by corporate leaders such as César Ritz, E.M. Statler, J.W. Marriott or Conrad Hilton (Figure 2.10), each of whom lent their names to both hotels and chains. This approach, with a business figure or celebrated host/manager (Fick, 2017) at its centre, is a continuation of an analytic approach that had long identified innovation with the acumen of specific 'leaders' and 'influencers' in the sector, and treated their lives and careers as the key structuring principle of hotel history narratives

Figure 2.10 Conrad N. Hilton, Habana Hilton opening press conference

(Lee, 1985; Nickson, 1997). In Florida's Gilded Age, Henry Flagler and Henry Plant are accorded primary importance in narratives of winter resort development as entrepreneurs who were engaged in the tourism sector more broadly (Braden, 2002; Graham, 2014; Revells, 2011). Charles Kemmons Wilson of Holiday Inn is credited with having pioneered a building style and a hotel form fusing innovative spatial configurations and forms of commercial hospitality that were singularly suited to the postwar age of the automobile (Jakle *et al.*, 1996: 261–285). Through an analytic focus on key entrepreneurs who financed, owned, and/or managed a hotel or chain, as well as those who were involved in drafting design and superintending construction, this approach tends to place a strong emphasis on entrepreurialism and leadership as critical to shaping hotels, their culture and hotel topographies.

Other scholars explore the hotel through the lens of the history of the firm, often situating it within wider industrial and service ecologies (e.g. Walton, 2014). Hotels are often seen as integral to commercial systems, but not always to industry; yet recently several studies have pinpointed how the hotel can nourish industrial development in a sustained and systematic way. Indeed, studies of hotels in different European contexts have underscored the extent to which the hotel served as a catalyst for industrialisation (Battalini & Fauri, 2009; Humair, 2011), generating demand for trades and infrastructure that produced important impetuses in a variety of manufacturing sectors, as well as in local financial services (Humair, 2011: 257). Cédric Humair (2011: 248), for example, explores the development of the hotel system in the Lake Geneva region from the 1830s, examines the interpenetration of the transport and hospitality sectors, and dissects how the hotel system played a critical role in stimulating local engineering, luxury goods and finance. Although he cautions that the hotel's role in spurring industrialisation must take into account local and regional ecologies, Humair produces a remarkable case study of this effect. Patrizia Battalini and Francesca Fauri (2009) affirm aspects of his findings about the relationship between the hotel sector and the wider economy in their study of Rimini. Studying the hotel in this light elucidates its key role in structuring commercial and economic relations, as well as the social and cultural fabric which has often been the focus of analysis. Exploring how systems of commercial accommodation, for example, are organised and operated as businesses – whether by individuals, families, limited partnerships, or limited liability companies – and how they are integrated with other enterprises, can advance the business history not only of commercial accommodation, but of the business matrix in localities and regions, and within the tourism, travel and hospitality sector more widely. Moreover, as we shall see in the next chapter, the analysis of the hotel within the context of integrated travel companies and multinational organisations illuminates strategies they adopted and pressures they faced in diverse geopolitical contexts, where their brand often served as a short-hand for a particular state.

Locating the Hotel

As these regional economic histories underscore, the spaces within which hotels are networked – and within which they are studied – are critical considerations in framing and evaluating their wider social, economic and cultural influences. A particular, primary 'area' usually bounds each hotel history, though they may also overlap – whether a transnational framework, a nation, a national political sub-unit, a city, a neighbourhood, or a region such New York's Adirondacks (Fick, 2017; Tolles, 2003), permitting scholars to explore its relation to a wider ecology. The choice of spatial framing, like chronology, is freighted with consequences for the narration of the hotel's functions and meanings. The preceding case studies explored hotels and regional economic contexts. Regional frameworks of analyses are common to many critical historical analyses. Others knit the local and the regional within national frameworks. Two of the most influential studies in this field are A.K. Sandoval-Strausz (2007) and Molly Berger's (2011) explorations of the American hotel's central role in national civic life, political development, commercial growth and the projection of power internationally. Sandoval-Strausz (2007) critically dissects a distinctively American hospitality culture shaped by its hotels. Sensitive to regional inflections, Sandoval-Strausz carefully maps the expanding hotel network, the waves of hotel buildings, and the expansion of hotel types onto a broader narrative of the ordering of American civic culture through these institutions, which also played a key role in shaping hospitality – the thorny set of ideas, ideals and practices connected to the provision of shelter, food and comfort to strangers. There is an underlying claim for an overarching *national* story, evinced in scholarship that stretches back decades (Boorstin, 1973, 1965). Annabella Fick (2017) has added an important, theoretically grounded perspective on spatial and social practices, using New York hotels as case studies for exploring the American hotel as she interweaves the local and the national. Other studies make the case for hotel culture as a distillation of a wider national culture: Richard White (2012) uses resorts to tease out the distinctive character of colonial Australian cultural, social and economic development, and to investigate how social relations there contrasted with those in the UK, and were materialised in resort forms, markets and travel practices. Other scholars favour different, overlapping frames: as we shall see, empire supplies a framework through which to apprehend forms of cultural, economic and social exchange operating at a transnational level. Chapter 5 highlights how tensions between the physical location of a hotel and the networks of which it is a part often make it vulnerable to conquest, either through acts of commandeering, or through obliteration.

Conclusion

These diverse, critical approaches to hotel history treat it as an institution capable of mutation and transformation, active in moulding the environment around it. It can shape economic ecologies, and configure social, political and cultural relations. To adopt a metaphor from the stage and screen – appropriately, given the extensive scholarship that has developed around the cinematic hotel (Clarke *et al.*, 2009) – the hotel does not just supply a setting for the elaboration of social and cultural relationships, or the application of new technology. It is a key performer with them, and it has been inextricably, dynamically and creatively engaged in these acts over many years.

This chapter explored the emergence of these sets of critical interests by charting the conventional meta-narrative of hotel development in western Europe and North America, with particular attention to the UK and the US. It also examined the contested relationship between the institutions of hotel and home, and has offered a basic typology of hotels and a discussion of key critical approaches to hotel history. The focus of hotel history has largely rested on the urban milieu, where the hotel is seen as a part of the signal shifts in the urban fabric in the 19th century that were linked not only to modes of production and divisions of labour in industrial capitalism, but also to new spaces and forms of social life (Knoch, 2008). The American palace hotel, for example, boasted a range of services and amenities, often from barbershops to luxury retail shops, that were associated with new regimes of urban consumption. Marvelling at the technologies of design, construction, and internal operation became a trope in contemporary narratives of the hotel's 'rise'. They have persisted to this day in structuring interpretations of hotel history. Alongside the urban milieu, technologies of transport play an outsize role in such accounts: the railway and the automobile, for example, are seen as key agents in the profound reorganisation of the infrastructure of travel, which had great impacts on the evolution of new institutional types of commercial accommodation, on their location, and on their relevance and obsolescence. The focus on these forms of locomotion, and on the hotel's urban contexts, however, tends to persistently occlude other relationships between technologies, institutions and places. The role of hotel labour, similarly, has attracted limited attention – perhaps owing to its enduring association with populations framed as 'marginal', as discussed in this chapter. In contrast, one of the key concerns in hotel historiography is the rise of the 'monster hotel' – pre-eminently in America, where modern systems and subjectivities struck observers as being tightly linked to the fortunes of the institution. Technology, rationalisation, efficiency and innovative business organisation have been studied as distinguishing hallmarks of American hotel history since the first decades that followed the founding of the republic.

3   The American Hotel

Western hotel history is grounded in an enduring narrative of American institutional and cultural distinctiveness, to which Anthony Trollope gave eloquent expression in the 19th century. He contended that grandeur of scale set American hotels apart from their British counterparts. In the New World, he commented '[e]verybody travels … the railways and the hotels have between them so churned up the people that an untravelled man or women is a rare animal' (Trollope, 1862: 557). The remarkable political experiment initiated by revolution, it seems, demanded a revolutionary form of lodging. Interest in charting its form has animated American hotel historians, amateur and professional, ever since.

Travelling at a time when inn nostalgia had yet to seize the English imagination, then reify and sentimentalise the English institution, Trollope (1862: 555) could couple his praise for the American hotel with a castigation of the solitary existence foisted on customers of inns in his native land. Unlike the long-inhabited rural realms of Europe, in America the hotel was, to Trollope, an early outpost of civilisation, anticipating other institutions. Hence it played an outsize role in forging the civic life of the country. He (1862: 556) noted that, in contrast to the wayside inns of small scale in England and in Europe, 'in the States of America the first sign of an incipient settlement is an hotel five stories high, with an office, a bar, a cloak-room, three gentleman's parlours, two ladies' parlours, a ladies' entrance, and two hundred bedrooms'. Yet for all of their impressive scale, and their public spaces, Trollope found the eating disagreeable, and the general 'mode of life' in such hotels unfavourable. He observed, for example, ways in which public rooms seemed to be mere extensions of the street, heaving with people with no other apparent connection to the establishment (1862: 564). These features of hotel life were alien to Trollope, and contributed to a binary construction of transatlantic hotel worlds that provided durable scaffolding for hotel historiography. The American hotel's incorporation within the urban streetscape in ways not paralleled in Europe has been regarded as a signifier of its unique openness and role as an anchor of civic culture. To Trollope it represented an unfamiliar permeability that unsettled his conventional understandings of the structures, uses and meanings of hotel space.

The core of Trollope's observations, if not the value-laden discourse within which they were enfolded, endured. In the 1930s, for example, the hotel historian Jefferson Williamson boldly declared that America's hostelries had borrowed nothing from the Old World, in a categorical formulation of national exceptionalism that traced the history of what he characterised as the 'most distinct of American institutions' (Williamson, 1930: 5). To Williamson, the American hotel was a beacon of civilisation on a new frontier. His narrative included many of the tropes of American hotel history: its singularity, its demotic character and its rise and mutability in line with the high mobility that epitomised the American experiment. The hotels of Chicago and of San Francisco, to Williamson, were materialisations of a teleological narrative of national, westwards expansion. The apotheosis of the exceptional scale, grandeur and technology of the American hotel was the 775-room Palace Hotel in San Francisco, opened in 1875 (Figure 3.1).

Daniel Boorstin (1965: 134–147) later re-stated these claims about the American hotel's singularity – effacing from his narrative, as Williamson had done, institutions in Europe, except those that had responded to, by mimicking, American innovations. The frame of critical analysis has now shifted to critically engage with how the American hotel assumed such a firm position at the vanguard of Western modernity. The American grand hotel remains a distinctive historical type, in the eyes of many scholars. Nicolas Fiévé et al. (2013: 7), for example, seek to clarify the distinctive features of the American hotel within a tripartite typology that marks its singularity:

(1) the American form, noted for its scale, central location and functional integration within both transport networks and other poles of urban activity;
(2) hotels at bathing and watering places associated with leisure and exceptional landscapes; and
(3) hotels, exemplified by those associated with the Swiss hotelier César Ritz, whose exclusive ethos and luxurious appointments deliberately evoke and indeed replicate the aristocratic social realm.

The overlapping character of these types is often evident in their historical evolution. Despite Williamson's and Boorstin's assertion, the American hotel had links to European institutions, but as both as an idea and as a form it has stood outside the parameters of European hotel

PALACE HOTEL AND LOTTA FOUNTAIN, SAN FRANCISCO.

5656. COPYRIGHT, 1901, BY DETROIT PHOTOGRAPHIC CO

Figure 3.1 Palace Hotel and Lotta Fountain, San Francisco, California, ca. 1900–1902

historiography. This is a point reinforced by the relative centrality of empire and colonialism to 19th-century European hotel histories, whereas the American hotel's 'global age' is charted in the second half of the 20th century and beyond. Hotel historians, even those whose interests have focused on tracing the diffusion of the grand hotel across borders, tend to endorse this view. The habit of living permanently within American grand hotels, and the convention of charging for food as well as board, drew comment and analysis for many decades, as observers puzzled over the character and origins of American hotel practices, as much as they marvelled at its scale and technologies. Interestingly, although the most recent literature on American hotel history treats the hotel as a critical infrastructure through which ideas of citizenship were articulated and social and economic identities were elaborated, many early sociologists offered a much glummer appraisal of the hotel's capacity to nurture good citizens and inculcate precepts of good citizenship. Their disquiet honed in on the peculiarly American practice of hotel living, but revealed wider anxieties about the hotel usurping the place of the middle-class home.

Place to Call Home or Palace of Pathology?

Early scholarship on American hotels, while remarking on the singularity of hotel life, often adopted a critical, and even pessimistic, stance in appraising the hotel as a landmark of modernity, in part because it was seared into American consciousness as a beacon of community, anchoring settler sociability, but not, it was hoped, to the detriment of more enduring and intimate institutions. When the young American sociologist Norman S. Hayner turned his attention to urban American hotels as the focus of his landmark PhD research in the 1920s, he grappled with questions that preceding writers had also asked – and which continue to animate scholars generations later. How did Americans inhabit the spaces of the hotel? How did they shape hotel spaces, and the hotel in turn shape them? How did the hotel crystallise peculiarly American cultural, social and commercial relations? To many commentators in the 19th and 20th centuries, the American hotel inhabited the urban landscape as a unique civic institution, knitted within the urban social world and the body politic in distinctive ways. They attached great importance to its spaces as public realms – albeit places whose access was delimited along gendered, racial and class lines. Early observers contended that if the American hotel was a product of America's remarkably peripatetic population and highly mobile culture, in the urban arena it highlighted essential conditions of modern life: a paying guest was reduced to a mere number and key. Individual personality was lost, and, as Hayner noted, guests 'are free, it is true, but they are often restless and unhappy' (1936: 1–2). The hotel had the potential to incubate civic consciousness and participation, but also anonymity and alienation, and even a disposition towards overstimulation and violence.

If the hotel could induce such unwelcome responses, observers puzzled over its relationship to the home, and, so doing, articulated concerns about the conflation of the hotel with domestic space. Was it a 'home away from home', or an anti-home, which defied the ideals of home ownership of the single-family residence (Berger, 2005b: 53), thereby unsettling prevailing ideologies of domesticity and space? Some American contemporaries felt that drawing a distinction between 'hotel life' and 'home life' was unhelpful: the modern hotel could supply many of the comforts of home, and also a suitable environment for social interaction (*The Caterer, Hotel Keeper and Refreshment Contractors' Gazette*, 15 January 1898, 22–23). Others regarded the hotel as a vessel of isolation and deracination – an institution that undermined precepts of *bourgeois* domesticity (Berger, 2005b: 52). It is this particular concern with the hotel as middle-class space – from the inception of the institution in the young republic – that nourished strong interest in its relationship to ideals of bourgeois domesticity. The distinctively American practice of living in hotels was increasingly prevalent, from the last quarter of the 19th century, among the urban middle classes in cities where private homes were the privilege of the wealthy (Dolkart, 2005: 15–17). There were practical motivations behind such strategies: the hotel supplied services otherwise provided by domestic servants at more modest cost for the middle classes (Hayner, 1936: 66–67). Yet despite these advantages, permanent hotel residency struck writers such as Norman S. Hayner (1936: 51–52) to be at odds with precepts of domestic life. The hotel could offer temporary accommodation away from home, but it could not displace the authentic domestic realm which anchored individuals to families, and families to neighbours, and knitted them within a broader civic culture. Hotels' salutary functions, in contrast to the home but also to the culture of hidebound, stuffy European institutions, lay in nurturing a Habermasian public sphere that built political identities, promoted commercial collaboration, and encouraged public sociability.

If hotel living expressed American modernity, it also forged a distinctive subjectivity. Norman S. Hayner contended that more people were making the hotel a permanent residence – smaller families in particular, but also people for whom it offered a kind of refuge, or for whom hotel amenities and conveniences were deemed especially valuable – widows and divorcees, for example. Hayner (1928: 787–788) also contended that the hotel was favoured by married couples that forsook children in favour of a companionate relationship – an aberrant configuration that was enabled by the hotel's socially insulating effects.

Concerns about the status of these denizens of hotels animated other contemporaries, including Robert Park (DePastino, 2003), who regarded the practice of hotel living as a pathway towards extinguishing citizenship. Hayner (1928: 793) invoked the term 'hobo' to denote the lack of social fixity that he associated with those women 'without vocation' who did not lend their energies to charities, social reform, or child rearing. But Park, developing his metaphor in a way that recalled Henry James, felt that the modern city exemplified the 'hotel life' writ large, with people living 'as the people do in some great hotel, meeting but not knowing one another', and substituting fleeting associations for the meaningful and grounded social interactions of small communities (in DePastino, 2003: 142). The social reformer Lawrence Veiller saw the denizens of the grand hotel and those of the lower-grade casual lodgings as sharing lifestyles, and inhabiting realms that impeded the inculcation and performance of good citizenship, both forsaking the grounding of family life for the liberties afforded by the hotel world (DePastino, 2003: 144). Hotels seemed natural points at which to stop on the way from one place to another, or to forge a public, civic culture. But as permanent sites of habitation, whether grand hotels or boarding houses, they could not substitute for more intimate institutions.

Norman S. Hayner's close intellectual links with Park, and his indebtedness to Georg Simmel's theories of mental life and the metropolis, are clear in his analysis of the hotel (Linder, 1996: 62–63). In exploring it as an institution of modern urban life, he was especially concerned with aberrant and transgressive behaviours that it nurtured. Hayner was by no means the first American to detect in this institution an especial distillation of national culture. Several decades earlier, Henry James offered his vision of the American 'hotel spirit'. To him, the hotel was the *ne plus ultra* of American culture. It was a place of apparently exuberant play and display, but also a site of extensive external supervision, whose demotic character was extinguished by crude commercialism, conventionality and the suppression of freedom (James, 1907). James regarded the American hotel spirit as a flamboyancy of display that masked regimes which effaced individuality and abolished the liberties of the home.

If Hayner's analysis took the form of sociological enquiry, his study was still very much a product of its age, betokened by his observations on the errant 'Hotel Child' – the supreme signifier of the ills of American hotel living. In life writing and fictional narratives, the experience of the hotel child often diverges markedly from the aberrant character Hayner represented (Fick, 2017), and even one of its most famous embodiments in popular culture, Kay Thompson's Eloise character, for all her mischief, displays none of the malignant traits that Hayner enumerated. Hayner denounced the practice of raising children within the confines of the hotel. It produced 'little actors' – tyrants of the corridors and hallways. Deprived of more suitable outdoor environments in which to play, some even accepted the kiss of 'strange men' in the lobby (Hayner, 1936: 119–131). In the hotel child, hotel living found the embodiment of its deepest pathology, exceeding even the isolated adult hotel dweller whose circumstances engendered a 'crabby and insistent' disposition (1936: 154). The vulnerable child was moulded not by the salutary influences of home, family and community, but by the impersonal and deracinating culture of the hotel. So much did the child signify the social ills of hotel life that Hayner (1936: 119–131) devoted a whole chapter to the figure.

The questions and concerns that animated Norman S. Hayner were not limited to American observers – or to American hotels, as the interwar meditations of Siegfried Kracauer reveal. But the distinctive propensity for 'living downtown' drew people of diverse resources and ranks into places initially designed for transient living, and fascinated, and unnerved, contemporaries. As Paul Groth remarks, the practices of hotel living were as varied as the places in which they were located: wealthy denizens of urban grand palace hotels inhabited 'social incubators' (Groth, 1994: 37) supplying a high-status address as well as high levels of mechanised and labour-saving services. The residents of rooming and boarding houses who shared facilites were often single, and the establishments themselves were segregated along racial, religious and occupational lines (Groth, 1994: 107). Outside these places were the cheap and largely male inhabited lodging houses characteristic of such districts as 'Skid Row'. As residential hotel life came to be bifurcated between the experiences of the denizens of the grand hotel and those of 'Skid Row', responses to the latter included the enforcement of moral, health and building codes and zoning regulations. Combined with patterns of suburbanisation and the elevation of the single family residence as an ideal for family and community health, outside the small number of people who continued to make grand hotels their homes after World War II, hotel residency was increasingly lived out in ageing buildings (Groth, 1994: 264). The substantial early sociological interest on the toxic potentialities of hotel life contrasts with more recent, critical scholarship which explores the American hotel as an arena in which ideas of citizenship were ordered, negotiated and forged. They tackle the thorny questions of how access to these 'palaces of the public' was structured in ways that produced a specific configuration of the public – and of public life – and promoted the hotel as a bastion of a form of citizenship that was delimited by class, gender and race.

Recent Perspectives on the American Hotel

Two landmark studies (Berger, 2011; Sandoval-Strausz, 2007) have explored the relationship between the American hotel and the political and economic contexts of 19th-century national development, building a strong critical framework for a new American hotel history. Whereas American hotel historiography was once largely narrated in a regional frame and exemplified by weighty, image-heavy depictions of resort regions, their new hotel history employs theory and case studies, evincing sophistication as it interprets the meaning of the hotel to American history, and the meaning of the American hotel to the wider world. It also departs from many of the pieties and platitudes of earlier studies, attempting to shake off the value-laden assessments of the 'dangers' of hotel life and the 'triumphs' signalled by America's hotel innovations, and emplaces the hotel within the study of hospitality and discourses of American progress and technology. In forging a new critical agenda for American hotel history, A.K. Sandoval-Strausz, who charts the emergence of interlocking cultural, social and economic processes that produced a distinctive form of *hospitality*, and Molly Berger (2011), who focuses on the technologies adapted within hotel space, position the hotel at the centre of histories of American liberal democracy, capitalism and cultural, social and technological development, not just at the turn of the 19th century and the early decades of the young republic, but also as industrial capitalism matured and as the 'hotel idea' was formulated (Berger, 2011).

Berger (2011) traces the American hotel in several major cities, as it developed within the context of innovations in design and construction, and reached its apotheosis in the modern skyscraper. She and many other scholars who collaborated on a special 2005 volume of the *Journal of Decorative and Propaganda Arts* seek to clarify the processes through which, as Berger contends, 'Americans "invented" the large urban luxury hotel in the early 19th century' (Berger, 2005a: 6). Much of her focus is on the design and construction of major urban hotels, and on the uses of space within them. The eastern seaboard's main commercial cities supplied America with its first sites of innovative hotel design and development. Establishments which are highlighted in these analyses contributed to a distinctive middle-class culture of sociability, consumption and politics, played out across the country, but perhaps most conspicuously in its largest cities. In the late 19th and early 20th centuries, New York City, with its high housing costs and dense environment, became a laboratory for inventive construction and design. Its soaring edifices joined beacons of financial progress that also boasted prominent positions in the New York skyline. Their interiors expressed traditional aesthetics and novel adaptations to the exigencies of space, designed by the architectural partnership of Schultze and Weaver: the Ritz, the Sherry-Netherland Hotel, the Hotel Pierre and the new Waldorf-Astoria (Dolkart, 2005: 19). The Waldorf-Astoria, in its 'old' and 'new' forms (the first is conventionally dated to 1893, the second to its opening in 1931 (Fick, 2017: 50)), boasted the famous Peacock Alley and Palm Garden (Figure 3.2), which telegraphed the hotel's claims to a singular hospitality (Dolkart, 2005: 38). In American hotel historiography, it has served as what Annabella Fick (2017: 18) describes as the 'grand hotel par excellence'.

French influence was discernible in the hotel's sumptuous rooms, which were deliberately furnished in the style of the most elegant 18th-century French and English standard (Dolkart, 2005: 40). In addition to exploring the hotel within discourses of opulence, technology and efficiency, Berger

Figure 3.2 Palm Garden, Waldorf-Astoria, ca. 1902

(2005b: 48) has elaborated on architectural programmes that united palace hotels and private residences in Gilded Age New York, exploring how the 'material world that they created served to shape, promote and reproduce economic and social relationships and the values that underpinned them'. In effect, social performances in palace hotels incorporated the middle classes within an urban social culture that reproduced those that played out in the private homes of the urban elite. New York has furnished hotel scholars with a laboratory to explore these performance codes (Fick, 2017). Their studies have revealed how these hotels were places in which the body politic developed, but was also heavily circumscribed.

Central to the scholarship are claims that the hotel form in America was neither derivative of European styles nor a receptacle and diffuser of their influences – but rather a distinctive, adaptive and agentive institution that responded to the unique demands of the American commercial and industrial middle classes, and to a particular idea of citizenship forged outside the sphere – some would say the constraints – of Old World social hierarchies. Gendered spaces and behaviours conditioned by those spaces interest historians treating the hotel as a site of ideological projection, production and reproduction. The hotel is treated as a network of discrete spaces, itself networked into wider environments, patterning production and consumption in which private and public spaces operate in complex, perhaps conflicting and sometimes complementary, ways. The logic behind hotel spatial ordering, and its ramifications, were highly conditioned along a number of axes. Rita Mazurkiewicz (1983), for example, in seeking to clarify the processes through which hotel spaces are historically gendered, identifies constraints on women's independent consumption within hotels, and relates them to historical processes of industrialisation that restricted female autonomy in public realms. Caroline Brucken (1996: 213–214), in contrast, identifies much broader ranges and forms of consumption, and contends that they offer ways of exploring female empowerment in the hotel. She welcomes the study of these patterns and processes as a counter-weight to narratives of transport, tourism and technological development that privilege male actors. Indeed, she identifies women as active and agentive figures in the 'hotel life' of antebellum America. Barbara Penner (2010), using the St Nicholas Hotel in New York as a case study, develops the argument that the urban luxury hotel was central to patterning 19th-century, middle-class consumption and that its interior spaces were adapted to gendered forms of consumption and sociability. Gendered taste and interests were critical to the design of hotel spaces and to middle-class cultures of display and consumption.

As a bastion of *bourgeois* public culture, the American hotel structured access and interactions along racial lines, institutionalising legal and cultural codes of segregation, but also providing space to challenge barriers to economic, social and political participation. Even Norman S. Hayner (1936: 37–38) observed the tendency of urban hotel geography to reflect patterns of racial segregation Adopting the lens of race to explore the hotel as a site in which the power of the law extended into the 'palaces of the public' to delimit different levels of access to the institution, A.K. Sandoval-Strausz (2007: 284–311) explores ways in which the Law of Innkeepers furnished a legal framework within which regimes of segregation in the American South were eventually challenged. He notes that the hotel operated in ambiguous ways in relation to the law, and the Law of Innkeepers became a focus for intense contest as a tool for either upholding or challenging racial codes in the civil rights era. Myra B. Young Armstead (1999, 2005) and Mark S. Foster (1999) have shown the ways in which colour bars historically operated to exclude African-American tourists in many hotels and resorts, including Saratoga Springs, both in terms of physical barriers to, and segregation of, facilities, and in the subtle textual effacing of their presence. This, in turn, created opportunities for African-American entrepreneurs to supply alternative accommodation and parallel entertainment venues. Travellers generated visual records that documented their experiences and, through them, mediated their claims to citizenship (Armstead, 1999, 2005). Many white-owned resorts also developed that targeted the black market (Foster, 1999). Annabella Fick (2017: 214) has used a case study of Harlem's Hotel Theresa to explore the institution of the African-American hostelry and tease out its role as a site and shaper of 'racial manifestation' through distinctive periods in the African-American experience, including the rise of black nationalism and the civil rights movement, affirming Jennifer Frong's (2006) findings that black-owned hotels became centres of African-American networking and sociability in a city whose institutions, unlike those of the South, operated under a regime of *de facto* segregation. They were also, she notes, sites of extensive external surveillance, which exacerbated class-structured tensions within the black population. Gender, race and class were central to ordering access to hotels, as well as to spaces within them (see Figure 3.3, which depicts African-American women war workers in the first hotel constructed to accommodate them, in an example of segregation on an institutional basis). They remind us that the study of the American hotel as institutions in which a public culture was forged requires scholars to attend to the ways in which those spaces were shaped by, and shaped, uneven participation in civic life.

American hotel history rests on the assertion that hotels were critical institutions in forging the identity of cities and bastions of nascent communities (Raitz & Jones, 1988). In grappling with the hotel as a 'palace of the people' that was an institutional bulwark of a democratic spirit, scholars have had to acknowledge and explicate the hotel's role in delimiting social and political participation along gendered and racial lines in particular, as well as supplying space for contest and revision. In the New World, the idea of the hotel as a foundational social institution marked an important distinction from the European hotel, which inhabited urban environments that already had a personality and pattern and manifested the conservative ethos of the aristocratic abode as a preceding institution. Habbo Knoch (2008) has explained this distinctive trajectory of American hotel development in terms of the enduring connections in Europe between the culture of the modern hotel and that of private accommodation, with its emphasis on private sociability. Unencumbered by the semi-aristocratic associations of the prestigious European metropolitan hotels, the American hotel still erected barriers to institutional participation, but as part of the distinctive context of its development, and in contrast to the

Figure 3.3 A group of young war worker-residents in a Washington, D.C. hotel, ca. Fall 1942 to April 1943

European hotels' abundance of labour, it embraced a culture of efficiency and technology with particular fervour. As both Sandoval-Strausz (2007) and Berger (2011) stress, the symbolism of the hotel as an organiser of American urban development, and its role as a marker of capitalist achievement, were starkly evident when individual establishments were officially opened, the events crystallised their roles in forging civic identities and ordering commerce and sociability in urban spaces.

Technologies and the American Hotel System

This idea of the pioneering civic role of an American institution that broke with the forms of the Old World through precocious technologisation has produced a genealogy of innovation associated with landmark establishments: the inaugural City Hotel in New York (1794), the iconoclastic Tremont House in Boston (1829), a marvel of technological innovation and an establishment dubbed both 'conceptually and typologically innovative' (Avermaete & Massey, 2013: 74), and the Astor House Hotel (1836). Many other leading hotels of their time add to an accreting narrative of expansion, experimentation and the forging of an urban, commercial system in the young republic: the St Nicholas in New York, for example, and the Eastern Exchange Hotel in Boston. These landmarks materialised advanced hotel technologies and provided a platform for ordering social life. Indeed, A.K. Sandoval-Strausz (2007: 43–44) invokes 'social technology' to conceptualise novel ways in which the American hotel organised people, with tangible results: a new standard of public accommodation, with expansive spaces for political expression, commerce, consumption and production – all building a 'new model of urban living'. The treatment of the hotel as a social technology is powerful; to understand how its creators sought to achieve these ends, we need to consider ways in which technology was applied to the science of hotel management, to the efficient, rational production of hotel space, and to its myriad operations, from moving people through it, to serving people meals, to attending to their physical comforts.

There was a rich metaphorical vocabulary to capture the size and complexity of urban American hotels in the 19th and early 20th centuries – from the 'city within a city' that captivated observers of a bewildering array of activities, to the 'monster' decried by its detractors, who saw it operating on an overwhelming, if not always terrorising, scale. Observers also often invoked the 'hotel system' as a metaphor to capture the hotel's interlocking functions and explore its mechanistic character. A mechanism is a potent metaphor that suggests concurrent routinisation, rationalisation and depersonalisation – all features of the systematised and highly ordered 'American hotel' at which some 19th-century observers marvelled, and others recoiled. The invocation of an integrated, well-oiled machine reflected the efficiency but also the impersonal character of an automatic contrivance. It also suggested how, in its ruthless efficiency, the hotel machine could efface the personality of the guest and host, and sharpen the transient, transactional character of their encounters.

The 'hotel system' often discursively demarcated qualities that contrasted with those of the Old World. The American hotel was as metaphorically deracinated from that realm as were the ceaselessly mobile people whom it served. Enhanced social and physical mobility, tireless industrial innovation, political ideals rooted in the triumph of the artisanate and the yeomanry: these characteristics marked the republic and nourished, and were nourished by, a fundamentally different hotel culture than that of Europe. As an institution, the hotel was integral to the urban landscape from its frontier origins, to the forging of the middle-class public sphere, to notions of luxury, social and technological advancement, and to the very idea of American progress itself, whether it was heralded by indoor lavatories or by electric lighting (Berger, 2011: 3). Technology is central to this wider narrative of progress. In exploring how it was adopted and received, Molly Berger critically expands Nikolaus Pevsner's (1976: 186) contention that '[t]he development of size and the development of style of American hotels is of sufficient interest to justify the pages devoted to them, but the most interesting aspect of hotel architecture in the United States is the development of equipment', from central heating to elevators.

Technological innovation has been regarded as critical to the patterning of hotel sociabilities. If the modern hotel furnished new prospects for liberating guests from the regimes of the home, it also bound them within new systems of sociability, surveillance and technology. Indeed, advanced levels of technologisation have long been seen as a significant shaper of American 'hotel life'. The American hotel and its technological regimes fascinated 19th-century writers such as George Augustus Sala (1861). As the hotel network extended its reach and grew in scale, its routines and regimes of registration, catering, accounting, employee management and guest surveillance combined to produce a form of commerce befitting a country rapidly churning with people, as unfixed physically as they were vociferous in their consumption and garrulous in their manner. A popular metaphor likened the hotel's internal systems to the body's circulatory system. Integrated front- and back-end operations relied on troops of people and countless machines, with pathways circulating people and information throughout the institution (Berger, 2011). These were characteristic of American establishments, but not exclusively so. Marc Katz (1999: 139) has noted that Siegfried Kracauer's meditations on the mediating role of the hotel lobby came as the hotel in Weimar Germany as elsewhere was becoming a central literary and cultural preoccupation, but also as European 'hotel space was instrumentalised by being made calculable, generic and thus potentially exportable' through the practices of Taylorism and the business structure of the chain. As London hotels grew in size and stature they evinced similar complexity, and evoked comparable observations. Take this example of the underbelly of the Hotel Cecil, described in evocative detail by one writer in 1898:

These modern palaces are marvels of artificial life ... To know how wonderful an organisation a modern hotel is, one needs, of course, to see much more than comes under his notice as a visitor. In some of the largest, indeed, to see the whole of it one would have to begin a good way off. The vast caravanserai just alluded to, for instance, situated in central London, has out in the suburbs its own modern farm, where it raises its own poultry, runs its own dairy, and grows flowers and shrubs and other things for decorative purposes, to the value, it is said, of something like £8000 a year – flowers and greenery alone! These things come jogging in by wagon and cart into a sort of goods depôt down in the basement of the vast pile towering up no less than twelve stories overhead. It is a strange, bewildering region of utilitarian ugliness – this nether world stretching away right and left from that stone roadway by which the vehicles come in; and one who has dropped down into it from the light and glittering splendour above will hardly fail to have Dante's Inferno suggested to his thoughts as he moves about the gloomy corridors, scales the bare, bleak, stone staircases, and passes from one to the other of the departments in which the Sybarites up in the realms above are being provided for. As one moves about the intricate labyrinth of kitchens and pantries, stores and engine-rooms, workshops and bakeries, he catches glimpses of a sort of under-world counterpart of the Elysium above – plainly furnished but comfortable sitting-rooms and dining-rooms and smoking-rooms, in which – not all together, for social status in this under-world is quite as real, if not as varied, as in the realms above – the various ranks of the staff are resting and getting a little social intercourse, or taking their meals at large and seemingly well-spread tables. (Modern Hotels, 1898: 673–674)

This vivid metaphor of 'artificial life' described a London establishment, but in America commentators contended that the vital organism reached its fullest form there. In fact, the tendency to homogenise American hotels in the interest of narrating their distinctive form endorses G.K. Chesterton's wry remark that '[b]roadly speaking, there is only one hotel in America' – a quotation with which Linda Pfueuller Davidson opens her study of standardisation in the American hotel system in the early 20th century (Davidson, 2005b: 73).

Davidson charts the adoption of efficiency-oriented practices in service, and also rationalisation in hotel design, reflected in hotel accounting, purchasing, registration and surveillance practices associated with nascent chains such as Statler and Bowman-Biltmore Hotels. They were also embedded within the very structure of the building itself, as the predominant aesthetic shifted in the period from 'Victorian eclecticism to Beaux-Arts classicism' (Davidson, 2005b: 74) and incorporated new ideas about interior circulation, as well as external structure and decoration. The putative distinctiveness of the American hotel was even more evident, scholars contend, when it became a laboratory for Taylorism and design innovation.

Innovations were evidenced by the application of Taylorist principles in now-iconic establishments such as the Hotel Statler in Buffalo and the LaSalle in Chicago (Mentzer, 2010). Statler Hotels manifested a particularly bold experimentation in the rationalisation of space, reflected in floor plans (Figure 3.4), in which rooms occupied equal space and access to amenities, and the materials of construction, rather than dictating the layout of the room plan, were adapted to it (Davidson 2005a, 2005b). These hotels, with the heightened logic of spatial organisation and differentiation between floors, catered to a broader socio-economic market than the lower-end rooming houses and the prestigious palace hotels that attracted so much commentary (Cocks, 2001). Through such innovations, historians contend that the American hotel was adaptive to the exigencies of modern life – uniquely so, in comparison with institutions in other places. Indeed, American innovations were notable in the progressive extension of the luxurious character of grand hotel space to new markets, even as the colour bar and other legal barriers regulated access to that hotel life.

American Hotels in the Era of Globalisation

The narrative of the American hotel's distinctive path, fuelled by a spirit of experimentation, the distinctive economic and social imperatives and resources of a frontier society, and freedom from Old World encumbrances, is reinforced as the focus shifts to the American hospitality sector's dominant position after World War II. An important dimension of American hotel history in the 20th century, and especially in the post-World War II era, was the expansion of its geographic compass. This development was a signifier of tectonic shifts in political and economic power, and also had far-reaching cultural implications. The extension of the American hotel beyond the country's shores was realised by its reach into colonial territory in the Philippines and Panama, in places such as Havana, and then, through the 20th-century American multinational corporation, into Latin America and the wider world (Quek, 2012; Wharton, 2001). It was grafted onto the vigorous projection of American

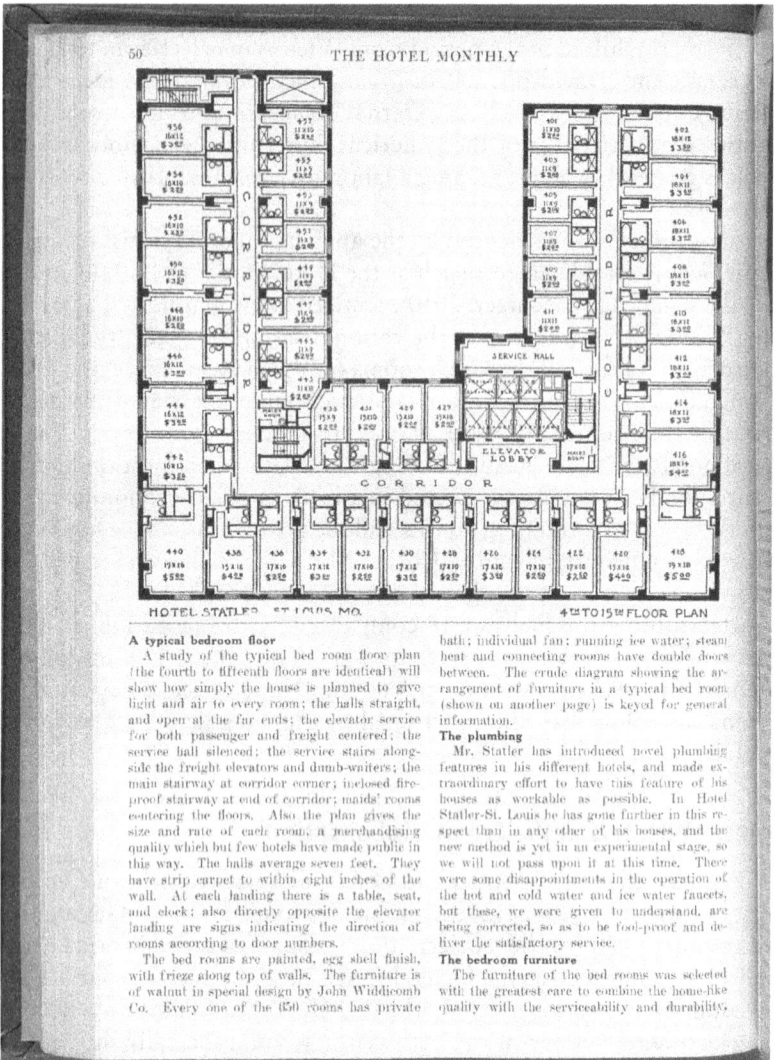

Figure 3.4 Hotel Statler, St. Louis, Missouri, fourth to fifteenth floor plan, 1918

political, economic and military power in the second half of the 20th century. The widespread identification of the American hotel as the benchmark for amenities and service quality in the sector in the post-World War II era, and the leading role of the Intercontinental Hotel Corporation and Hilton Hotels International, Inc. in the internationalisation of the American hotel, was significantly enabled by the American government's efforts to promote tourism as an engine of economic recovery in postwar western Europe. These efforts were supported by European governments (Quek, 2012) and were accompanied by increasing American tourist traffic and improved incomes generally. Although Stan Luxenberg's (1985) history of the franchise system is an excoriating critique of its economic, social and even cultural impacts, other scholars have taken a less categorical stance. Often a hotel's success in international commercial hospitality reflected the firm's organisational nimbleness, enabled by minimal capital investment in risky climates through management contracts and limited direct ownership (Quek, 2012). When the Habana Hilton fell into Fidel Castro's hands during the Cuban Revolution, for example, the symbolic monumentalism of the (albeit belated) seizure of a beacon of American capitalism in the capital city of the new revolutionary state was only faintly reflected in Hilton International's bottom line (Merrill, 2009: 141–176).

The Intercontinental Hotel Corporation (IHC) exemplified a shift in business structures and strategies as American hospitality entered new markets, especially those in which American political interests were given priority by the state, and also marked the continuing identification of the American hotel as setting the benchmark for comfort and amenity. Mary Quek (2012: 206), in her study of the IHC, draws attention to the critical role of political environments in fostering the conditions conducive to the hotel sector's expansion (as a division of Pan-American Airways), and in the postwar period identifies the European Recovery Plan and the International Civil Aviation Agreement (1941) as critical factors in the development of that environment. Consumer growth and preferences also played their role, as did the advent of the jet – a technological development that helped to propel internationalisation in both the airline and hotel divisions of the company (Quek, 2012: 212). The IHC's frustrated experience in Latin America compared to Europe reflected a more challenging political environment and investment climate. The company's strategies for internationalisation included: (1) limiting exposure through the use of management contracts, rather than outright ownership, which constituted part of a 'hybrid' model of entry into foreign markets that contrasted with the strategy followed by many manufacturers at the time; (2) the extension into Europe in the 1960s after its Latin American forays; and (3) exploiting locational advantages conferred by sympathetic host and home governments. Although its reliance on management which was more familiar with the airline than the hospitality sector created difficulties (Quek, 2012: 213–216), its eventual success in establishing a world-wide network rested in part on the logic of pursuing the hotel business as an airline subsidiary. Quek's study argues that American leadership in the sector was a consequence of its adaptation to the logic of the market – and also cites critical political contexts connected to American political hegemony, which facilitated overseas business development.

The post-World War II American hotel, when exported to the metropolises of former European colonial powers, and to cities in newly decolonised states, also had inscriptional potency in marking its place in the new international order. When, as was the case with many of the Hilton International hotels explored by Annabel Wharton (2001), the hotels came to dominate the skyline and dwarf colonial-era hotels, the expression of new power relations through the transformed hotelscape was unequivocal (Wharton, 2001: 4). Hilton International played a critical role both in consolidating and extending the 'American' brand into many corners of the world in the era in which formal decolonisation began – and also in former *métropoles*, such as London (Czyzewska & Roper, 2017). It was deeply involved in the ideological struggles of the Cold War, as America sought to craft a world order through the agency of both soft and hard power. Wharton (1999) has sketched a highly instructive continuum between the colonial hotel and that of the Cold War era – exploring 19th-century institutions in major European capitals, designed by Europeans in a neoclassical style – Pera Palas in Istanbul, Shepheard's Hotel in Cairo and the Grande Bretagne in Athens – through the end of World War II. She charts the ways in which Hilton International participated in the construction of new hotels in several cities – institutions whose design, locations and technological features constituted 'dramatic' interventions (Wharton, 1999: 291) in the urban landscapes. The new hotel topographies can be read (and were interpreted at the time) as projections of American power and entrepreneurial capitalism, as well as an 'aestheticized technological efficiency' (Wharton, 2001: 6) that imbued all aspects of the hotels' outward appearances and internal operations. It marked a sharp shift from the aesthetics and interior spatial regimes of colonial-era hotels.

Wharton (2001: 4) argues that the erection of a new hotel often signalled the eclipse of a colonial-era hotelscape. The newer hotels married American consumerist and design ideals in bold shows of modernity that were signified by the promiscuous use of plate glass in their construction. The glass showcased design technology and became part of a critical component of the hotel-as-spectacle through ideals that were rendered legible to guests and also to those outside the hotel. The inhabitation of the hotel became highly conspicuous to those inside and outside its walls, projecting the meaning of American consumer culture beyond them. Thus, Wharton shows that the orientation and position of the Hilton often contrasted markedly with those of the grand hotels which they symbolically eclipsed, and also physically dwarfed. The design of, and construction materials used in, the new Hilton hotels proclaimed new geopolitical power relations. In Istanbul, for example, the technologies of double-pane glass and air-conditioning, and the absence of the old grand-hotel affordances of the tea-room doors, insulated guests from the city's sensorial onslaught (Wharton, 2001: 27). In Cairo, plans for the Nile Hilton (Figure 3.5) began shortly after the colonial-era Shepheard's Hotel had been razed by a mob (Wharton, 2001: 32). The distinctive form of the US hotel in these global sites reflected its social role and processes of entrepreneurial commoditisation. The structuring and programming of space within it was linked to its importance as an investment producing returns. It also transfigured the American hotel into a new signifier of global power, just as technology had marked the distinctiveness and structured the meaning of the American hotel in the previous century.

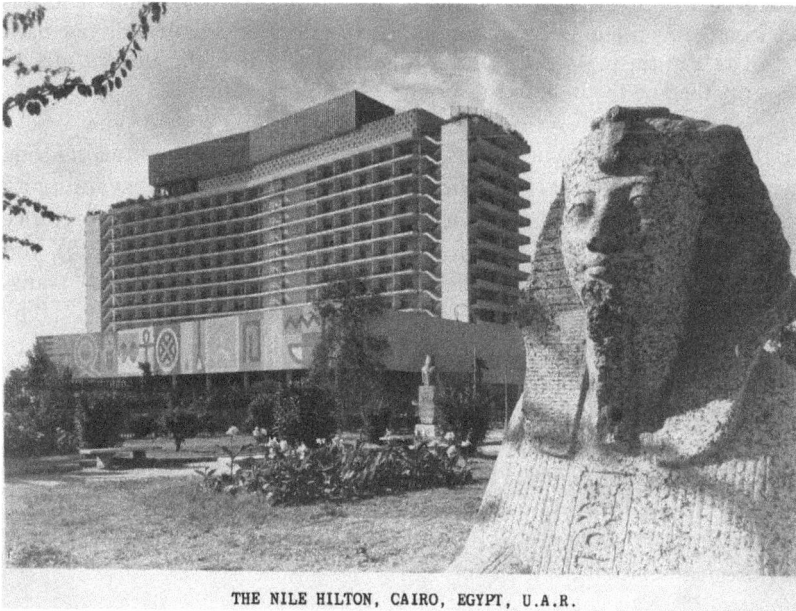

THE NILE HILTON, CAIRO, EGYPT, U.A.R.

Figure 3.5 The Nile Hilton, 1961

Conclusion

Scholarship on the 20th-century American hotel extends the study of its singularity, which in the 19th century rests on its status as a citadel of middle-class endeavour and of technological experimentation, as it explores its forms of spatial rationalisation and multinational operations. If the story of America's international hotel age privileges a later period of global capitalism from that of European colonialism (making it a laboratory for the political economy of late capitalism (Levander & Guterl, 2005: 5–6)), the global footprint of the European colonial hotel preceded it. In light of the emergence of new hotel forms in an American-dominated postwar international order, there emerged a palpable nostalgia in some corners of hotel historiography for colonial establishments. Coffee-table books lamented the demise of the colonial-era hostelry:

> Others of the great hotels stand yet, but changes of regime have turned them into empty shells. Who today would turn aside for a spell at the *Shah Abbas* in Isphahan, that admirable 17th-century caravanserai converted into a luxury hotel? Who would want to stay at that hotel in Tripoli, a vestige of colonialism which until recently was run by Italians just as well as it ever was before the war? And who, finally, will ever revisit the hotel at Angkor, the *L'Auberge des Ruines*, where it stands isolated by the jungle and dominated by tall trees, from which one used to gaze at the prodigious ruins of the great temple in the glow of sunrise or bathed by the light of the moon? (Grèce, 1987: 10)

To these institutions, Michel de Grèce added the Peninsula Hotel in Hong Kong, which, 'despite its brilliant colonial past' had suffered the indignity of miniaturisation amidst the city's soaring skyscrapers, whose presence signified far more than a transformation of the cityscape (1987: 10), and extolled the 'small and marvellous' Claridge's in London, which 'transports its guests instantly and totally to the era of the Raj' (1987: 11). The rise of the multinational American hotel chains signified the eclipse, to him and to others, of the European colonial project, and the emergence of a new programme which projected American power, with its own aesthetic and service culture, and distinctive institutional forms (Wharton, 2001: 2). The colonial hotel has attracted interest from historians as more than a vestigial institution, however: critical scholarship now emphasises its complex and malleable forms and symbolisms, during and after the era of European colonialism.

4   The Colonial Hotel

Colonialism supplies a critical framework within which European hotel history is studied, and the inscriptional power of the Western hotel in many milieus is explored. To the semiotician, the hostelry can serve as a physical signifier of colonial projects, offering a window onto political, cultural, social and economic relations worked out in the spaces of colonial environments. This set of interests, and their chronologies, have tended to erect key thematic and chronological distinctions between European and American hotel historiography. America's colonial era began later than that of European states such as Britain, France, Spain, Portugal and Italy, and the vigorous extension of its hospitality sector generally coincided with the period of formal decolonisation.

Theoretical directions in literary and cultural studies have offered new frameworks to explore the colonial hotel beyond seeing it as a vehicle for the diffusion of European cultural, commercial, or architectural forms, or consigning it to obsolescence in the postcolonial era. Indeed, postcolonialism has nurtured scholarship that highlights its adaptive symbolisms and material forms. Responding to its theoretical insights and priorities, and to tourism history's deep engagement with colonial-era travel practices, from big-game shooting to archaeological tours, historians have questioned the extent to which the colonial hotel was truly sealed off from its broader environment, offering mainly European guests a site of cultural familiarity within which they could 'retreat' from foreign surroundings. Many have meticulously unpacked relations of race, ethnicity, gender and socio-economic status that played out within the institution, seeing them as patterning complex interactions. Emphasising that colonialism took many forms in different parts of the world, they have also dissected the meanings of the hotel form – its structure, interior spatial organisation, décor and exterior ornamentation. They find evidence that destabilises the concept of the hotel-as-metropolitan-enclave and instead underscores its hybridity. And they invite us to see it as a mediating space between genders, classes and cultures, and also between global and local interests.

The Hotel and the Colonial Project

Outside Europe, the construction of hotels in areas where European travellers, political authority and capital penetrated is often narrated as an extension of the European hotel system. Like the American hotel, hotels in European empires assumed many forms – made of various materials, on a range of scales, with a diversity of aesthetic elements, interior organisations, functions and markets. In many cases hotels are seen as marking a European power's footprint in the colonies – indeed, it could become a formal node in networks of colonial administration (the King David Hotel in Jerusalem, for example, functioned as the headquarters of the British mandate authority in the 1940s), and a site of technological diffusion (Peleggi, 2012: 133). Adopting a perspective common to many chroniclers of colonial hotels who interpret them as essentially external institutions transplanted to non-Western areas, Andrew Humphreys (2011: 15) argues that they constituted 'outposts of Europe planted on Egyptian soil' that anchored 'European enclaves' and offered few aesthetic concessions to their environment. This perspective largely evaluates them as part of the fabric of colonial cities, as institutions and urban landscapes were configured according to the priorities of the *métropole*. Its interest lies in explicating ways in which the dominant colonial power, and colonial capital, ordered the social and economic environment of the colonial city. There are many places where evidence of this influence is indisputable. As elsewhere – even in popular Grand Tour-era hostelries – many hotels displayed a marked preference for English and French names, often combining the two, as in the ubiquitous 'Hôtel d'Angleterre', which telegraphed their aspirations and also their strategies to capture lucrative European market segments (Humphreys, 2011: 16) Anthony D. King, in charting the dissemination of colonial grand hotels, contends that hotels were entwined with imperialism, and lay at the heart of a colonial urban system. They were deeply implicated in the growth of the scale of transnational imperial commercial networks, flows of people and circulations of capital, and signalled what Maurizio Peleggi characterises as the 'mobility of colonial life' (Peleggi, 2012: 152). Indeed, King notes that when the blueprint of late 19th-century European colonialism in Africa was agreed at the Congo Congress in 1884, the continent was carved up among European powers at Berlin's Grand Hotel Alexanderplatz (King, 2016: 149).

Interpretations of the relationship between the colonial hotel and its host environment have tended to bifurcate: some are primarily interested in the hotel as a Western institution implanted in colonial realms, tied to the political, economic and cultural authority of the imperial state and with its efforts to inscribe authority on the landscape. Others treat the hotel as a site of mediation, contest and contact. The colonial grand hotel looms large in scholarship on colonial *tourism* especially – often eclipsing other functions, and obscuring other forms of commercial accommodation, while generating a substantial body of commemorative literature. Its interests are often weighted in favour of exploring the colonial grand hotel as a site designed for European leisure practices abroad, where social solidarities were forged among the colonial elite in a building whose form projected the power of the *métropole* onto the colony.

Cairo's Hotelscape

Given the scope and scale of European imperialism, there is no dearth of sites in which to explore the erection of the colonial hotel alongside other institutions. In Egypt, for example, the European presence grew after Napoleon's invasion, spurred by interest in the relics of Antiquity and later by a seasonal influx of northern Europeans who favoured it as a winter resort (Humphreys, 2011; Lyth, 2013: 184). Although the famous British tourist company Thomas Cook and Son arrived in the country after 1860, Martin Anderson has shown that a substantial elaboration of a tourism infrastructure preceded that date. (Anderson, 2012: 260). In fact, prior to Cook's arrival, the European's Egyptian tour had embraced the Nile Cruise, the offices of the 'native' dragoman and immersion in Egyptian culture through transport on a putatively indigenous conveyance – the *dahabiya* (Lyth, 2013: 180–182). Later, Cook, whose Egyptian office was established at the iconic Shepheard's Hotel, invested heavily in hotels, breaking with its system of issuing, as a third-party, coupons that could be redeemed at eligible places of accommodation in established resorts (Hunter, 2004). The opening of the Suez Canal in 1869 transformed tourists' relationship to Egypt, and spurred the expansion of an infrastructure of hotels to supply an increasingly high volume of traffic, much of it developed under the aegis of Thomas Cook's son, John Mason Cook (Lyth, 2013: 183–186). The sector received crucial support from Egypt's leader, Muhammad Ali, in what Anderson (2012) charts as a period of tourism's internationalism, as British tourists in particular pushed the boundaries of leisure travel beyond the borders of Europe into and beyond the Mediterranean. The infrastructure accommodating them expanded beyond the traditional places made available through British and Egyptian officials (Anderson, 2012: 262). Under Ali's grandson, Ismail Pasha, the physical infrastructure of Egypt, from the Suez Canal, to resort hotels, to the Italian Opera House, reflected the penetration of

European capital, the increasing influence of the British state over the country's administration, and Egypt's integration within the British global tourist network (Scham, 2013). Indeed, James Moore (2014) has used hotels as indices of the city's morphology. Moore charts their development in places such as Ismailiyah as he traces Cairo's complex and varied patterns of suburbanisation to develop a much more nuanced interpretation of the city's expansion than the 'dual cities' model. That model is premised on the parallel and spatially separate development of Western-influenced and 'traditional' urban forms and communities in places such as colonial Egypt and India.

One of many caveats to studying hotels and the infrastructure of commercial tourism generally in the non-West during the era of Western tourism is that the growth of hotels was not limited to colonial possessions, protectorates, or countries under *de facto* European control, such as Egypt. Thierry Sanjuan *et al.* (2003) have explored grand hotel topographies in several such areas of Asia. In Meiji Japan, for example, the Imperial Hotel, built in 1889, signified both a deliberate programme of economic and social modernisation and extensive Western contact on the urban landscape, reflecting the formation of new networks of people, goods and ideas in its realisation (Fiévé, 2003: 48), and offering a stage for elite sociability. Earlier in the Meiji restoration (from 1869), Japan developed a railway network, witnessed the erection of new hotels in major urban centres financed with Japanese capital, and accorded much greater freedom of commerce and travel to Western powers. There, hotels were signifiers of a Western-influenced modernity in a Japanese idiom that was formulated and implemented by Japanese actors. In China, grand hotels in the European style, including the Hotel Astor in Tianjin, dating to 1863, are regarded as signifying the robust economic power of the European powers in their coercively-extracted concessions (Sanjuan, 2003). They had counterparts in formal colonial possessions such as Macau, where hotels which adopted Portuguese forms and names reflected the influence of the *métropole* over their form (Figure 4.1). Meanwhile, in one of the world's most expansive non-Western empires, the response to intensified European travel in, and commercial contact with, the Ottoman Empire was reflected in the geographical distributions of lodgings, in their operations, and in their forms.

The Hotelscapes of Jerusalem and Constantinople

Urban centres in the Ottoman Empire developed hotel topographies that reflected the diversity of their populations, the comingling of cultural

Figure 4.1 Macau, exterior of Pousada Inn, 1950s

influences, and the growth of traffic from the West. In their study of the hotel and tourism sector in Jerusalem, for example, Shimon Gibson *et al.* (2013) note that demand for accommodation grew along with the number of Western travellers in the Ottoman-ruled city. They chart the emergence of an infrastructure to meet their needs. Some, but not all, Europeans participated in longstanding practices of devotional travel, while others naturalised it as part of an increasingly popular leisure tour of 'The East' (Gibson *et al.*, 1-2). Locational preferences (in relation to the city gates and consular buildings (Gibson, 2013: 17)) and comfortable and familiar amenities distinguished these sites. The network of hostelries expanded to meet the requirements of the Western traveller. In Christianity's holiest city, the heavy presence of diasporic communities and Christian Palestinians in the hotel trade underscored their critical role in mediating between these consumers and the dominant host culture. Hotels in cities such as Istanbul (Constantinople) responded to, and shaped, the shifting travel preferences and practices of the Western tourist market by developing and adapting lodging forms. Like the diasporic and Christian Arab hoteliers, people drawn from ethnic and religious groups played key cultural brokerage roles through their presence in the hotel sector.

Nineteenth-century Istanbul has attracted scholarly interest for ways it developed and adapted forms of commercial accommodation for Western tourists in the 19th century, during a period when volumes of trade and human passenger traffic expanded (Arslan & Polat, 2015; Gibson *et al.*, 2013). As in Jerusalem, diasporic communities such as Levantines were critical to the development of Istanbul's accommodation network, underlining their authority as mediators between the host environment and hotel guests (Arslan & Polat, 2015: 104). The 'Western' hotel form was most firmly elaborated in the districts of 19th-century Istanbul strongly associated with a strong, diasporic Christian presence – in particular Galata and Pera (Beyoğlu). Galata had historically served as a Genoese enclave within the city. Likewise, Pera, on the city's European side, had evolved by the 19th century to become a principal commercial, cosmopolitan and elite residential district. Its development was strongly influenced by European architectural aesthetics and cultural styles (Tellan, 2016). Elif Bayraktar Tellan challenges the orthodox interpretation of hotel development in Istanbul, which traces the modern Istanbul hotel to the era of Westernising, *Tanzimat* reforms beginning in 1839 (which included substantial changes to building codes and urban layouts). Instead, she identifies critical developments in commercial accommodation prior to the 1840s, with the rise of guesthouses from the 1810s, predominantly operated by Italians and Levantines, for European travellers. These institutions, which had their own hierarchy of status and clientele, were distinctive from previous forms, such as the *khan*, which operated outside a strictly commercial framework, though they retained personalised features of attendance that may have marked them as distinct from modern 'hotels'. They in turn were adapted from the 1840s into recognisable hotel forms, alongside newly built hotels such as the Hôtel d'Angleterre (Tellan, 2016: 142). The city's main hotel district was also the location of its most famous 'grand hotel'. Designed by a French architect, Alexandre Vallaury, built in the 1890s, and owned by a French company, the Pera Palas, which Annabel Wharton (2001: 16) describes as a 'generic neo-Renaissance' edifice, instantiated European ideas of the East through a familiar eclectic aesthetic that employed neo-Turkish decorative elements (Wharton, 2001: 16–17). The analysis of the material form of colonial hotels has offered scholars a way of exploring intersecting colonial and indigenous influences over the establishments.

Analysing the Hotel in Colonial Environments

There is certainly evidence, whether in built form, sources of capital, internal spatial organisation, technologies, and even restaurant menus, to support the claim that hotels in non-Western environments manifested European influence and marked European power. Hotels in Egypt and elsewhere visibly reflected European tastes, and also transmitted ideologies and practices of leisure, business and health-related travel, however much they were influenced by local conditions. Elements of spatial organisation, service culture and amenities cued travellers to the enduring influence of the *métropole*. Sometimes the very materials with which the hotel was erected signalled that influence in narratives of technological and technical transfer. In tracing the building biography of Watson's Esplanade Hotel in Bombay through the lens of construction history, for example, Jonathan Clarke (2002) has shown how a metropolitan network played an especially crucial role in the hotel's realisation. The network comprised Rowland Mason Ordish as engineer, the Phoenix Foundry Company in Derby, and John Hudson Watson, a colonial entrepreneur. Under their coordinated supervision, components of the hotel's innovative, modular iron-skeleton frame structure were designed and produced in England, and exported for assembly in Bombay (Clarke, 2002). Clarke traces the hotel's relative positioning within the network of colonial hostelries, from its opening in 1871 to its expansion in 1888, to its eclipse at the turn of the century, and its decline into a now-crumbling mansion. The longitudinal analysis illuminates how the now-shabby Esplanade Mansion began its life on a drawing board not only as a proposed prefabricated office and showroom that evolved into an iconic hotel, but also as 'the first multistorey habitable building in the world in which all loads, including those of the brick curtain walls, are carried on an iron frame' (Clarke, 2002: 18). Clarke proposes a technological genealogy of the modern skyscraper that accords primacy to a colonial hotel that was obscured in the decades after its erection by Bombay's building boom, and is now little known. So doing, he interweaves the building's biography with a study of urban morphology, revealing important dimensions of technological transfer and colonial urban development in a case study that reveals how materials and knowledge were transported from *métropole* to colony, while also demonstrating how meanings and uses evolved over time.

The built form of the hotel could proclaim imperial power in potent ways, if not always as dramatically and unambiguously as in late 19th-century Bombay. In America's Philippines possessions, David Brody argues that the Manila Hotel was part of a programmatic effort to inscribe a colonial modernity in the landscape – one that was conceived to displace a colonial style associated with the vanquished Spanish rival. The hotel, while being structurally adapted to the climate, nonetheless was envisaged within a wider project designed to telegraph Western power (Brody, 2010: 140–163). It is tempting to treat such establishments as stark exclamations of metropolitanism – and to see them as citadels of colonial power and sites of an insular, even ossified, colonial culture. This is especially the case in the interwar period – which is often identified as an era of gentle decline for many of the grand hotels of Europe, when they appeared to stubbornly resist changing metropolitan social codes, and displayed a supposedly marked obliviousness to events unfolding on, and transforming, the continent. But colonial hotels were conceived, built and operated within the context of diverse imperial ideologies.

In a study of architecture and tourism in Italian colonial Libya, for example, Brian McLaren (2006) uses hotel architecture to tease out complex relationships between the built form and the ideologies of Fascist-era tourism and imperialism. The priority that guides his reading of the colonial-era hotel network's development is to clarify how it enabled travellers to consider themselves as participating, to some extent, in a form of escapist leisure – as participants in an authentic, primitive indigenous culture (which was inevitably a Western construction) as they travelled through unfamiliar environments, while at the same time participating in a colonial system that extended comforts and familiarity into the colonial milieu (McLaren, 2006: 105–106). In some respects, he pursues an agenda that is germane to the study of lodging in many colonial networks – the development of a French 'hotel system', for example, has also been seen as critical to providing both a material infrastructure for travel and an ideological infrastructure for empire (Hunter, 2007). But in Italy, with different political incentives, and a different historical relationship to the colonised space, the hotel building programme assumed a unique salience, and hotels assumed an equally distinctive form. The project in which Libyan colonial tourism was implicated was what McLaren describes as 'Fascist modernity' (McLaren, 2006: 109). It involved two Orientalist frames – that of Romantic exoticism, and that of scientific research investigation, including ethnographic surveys of Libyan populations, especially Berbers, which became a template for structuring the tourist experience in Libya, as well as an instrument validating the colonial project (McLaren, 2006: 118–120).

Hotels, notable for an architectural syncretism and design eclecticism (Von Henneberg, 1996), were enlisted in structuring this experience as mediating institutions, forming part of a 'coherent system' through which tourists experienced Libya (McLaren, 2006: 130, 158–162). Grand hotels' built forms in colonial Libya assembled a variety of motifs in an architectural eclecticism that reflected the absorption of indigenous influences into an (albeit dominant Italian) aesthetic that reflected a dialogue between styles. Their forms materialised colonialist ideas of indigeneity through selective representations of a design 'vernacular' (McLaren, 2006: 131). As *bricolages*, these buildings and the hotel network epitomised an Italian architectural discourse that was deeply informed by the politics of Fascist colonialism. Different sites of Italian colonialism – Libya and Ethiopia, for example – occupied markedly different positions within those politics, in part owing to ways they were interpreted in relation to Italy's ancient past. Design principles also changed as the ideological underpinnings of Fascist imperialism evolved.

By the early 1930s, the architectural discourse had evolved to embrace a vision of Libyan architecture that framed indigenous forms and styles as historically and essentially Roman, and therefore linked inextricably to the *métropole*. The hotels, McLaren (2006: 180–181) contends, fused 'indigenous Libyan architecture with a quintessentially modern language' producing a project that was 'at once indigenous and modern, local and supra-regional'. What distinguished the Libyan example was an interpretation of the colony as an integral part of an historic territory over which Rome had claimed dominion: hence the blurring of narratives between the past and the present and between indigenous and exogenous styles into a master narrative that united colony and *métropole*. This was a bold formulation that effaced Arab influences in favour of forms that buttressed Italy's claims to 'reclaim' its historic presence in, and assert it contemporary power over, Libya. The colonial hotel manifested this ideology in built form, but not as a replication of metropolitan forms.

Enclave or Site of Encounter?

If the conception, erection and uses of hotels advanced colonialist ideologies in places such as Libya, they were sites of imbrication between the local and the extra-local, betokened by ornamental eclecticism and by the assimilation of a variety of architectural styles. As much as the colonial hotel's functions may appear to have supported technological and cultural transfer in one direction, there are many ways in which it operated as a site of negotiation, however unequally the encounters were ordered along axes of socio-economic status, gender and race. The result of a recent emphasis on hybridity and mediating spaces of cities and of empire has been a consideration of the porousness and permeability of supposedly enclavic colonial space. This is attributable in large part to the wider interest in colonial history and in postcolonial studies, which has helped to de-centre perspectives on colonial institutions and problematise conventional understandings of how the *métropole* ordered social, cultural and economic authority.

Examples of hybridity, and of local participation in the spaces and cultures of the hotel, are not hard to find. In Egypt, for example, asymmetrical power relations did not negate the agency of locals in the creation of hotel culture (Hazbun, 2007). In parts of colonial New Zealand, Maori participated directly in hotel ownership, and were actively involved in the development of a key tourist district through strategic deployments of capital and labour (Bremner, 2013). We have seen the critical role played by ethnic and religious intermediary groups in hotel operations in many 19th-century cities. These examples shade and qualify understandings of the colonial hotel as European implantation in the landscape.

Complex sociabilities were also contested within the spaces of colonial hotels. In the post-World War II years, for example, John Flint (1983) has found evidence of a conservative racial hotel culture operating in British West Africa, with the tacit support of the colonial administration there. A minor scandal erupted when the Hotel Bristol in Lagos upheld a colour bar against a senior black colonial administrator; it revealed a gulf in sensibilities between public opinion in Nigeria and its Governor (who, while deferring to the ban, insisted that official institutions forbade such actions), and between the Governor and reformist colonial office figures in London. The episode revealed internal tensions within the colonial administration, and challenges interpretations of racial politics of British West Africa that contend that they were unproblematic, compared at least with those of eastern and southern Africa. Colonial hotels were also spaces of contest over racial codes and identities. Ruth Craggs (2012), for example, argues in her study of hotels in 20th-century Southern Rhodesia that hotels were sites where colonial ideologies were both constructed *and* challenged. The hotels of Salisbury supplied space in which exclusive colonial settler sociability and class-conditioned, gendered and racialised identities were iterated and reiterated (Craggs, 2012: 219–220). Craggs contends that hotels were historically central to 'political geographies in different registers' – as symbolic landmarks, as sites of sociability, and as privately owned places that were 'public' in many respects, but whose public was created, maintained and contested under legal regimes. In Southern Rhodesia, the 'colour bar' was enacted and challenged in hotels, which became critical places: (1) where codes that enacted 'European sociability' through racial exclusion at different levels were produced; (2) where those codes were challenged (Craggs, 2012: 215); and (3) where, as coded hospitality space and places of international circulation, the contested racial politics of Southern Rhodesia became visible and known to a wider international public. Craggs treats the hotel as a space that both operates within and stands apart from the institutional and ideological frameworks that define and maintain racial separation – and suggest its subversive potentials. Some of Salisbury's old colonial grand hotels offered a place for the articulation of a liberal multi-cultural political identity after 1959, when the strictures of the 'colour bar' were loosened, and where, in contrast to Lagos's 'Hotel Bristol' incident, various actors tested the capacities of commercial hospitality to undermine policies of racial segregation.

Maurizio Peleggi has developed a valuable conceptual framework within which to understand the complex operations and status of colonial hotels. The era of high imperialism, he writes, 'furnished the political stability, material infrastructure and ideological superstructure' to support the extension of the compass of travel (2012: 125). He contends that, from food, to entertainment, to technologies, such hotels had the amenities and capacities to become 'comfort zones' that supplied familiar regimes and commodities to travellers. Many, implanted in as far-flung places as Rangoon and Cairo, came to symbolise the European colonial project and shared a common set of aesthetic and functional roles. They also supplied a site where technologies such as electricity were first applied in colonial settings, and therefore served as places of metropolitan diffusion. The colony was knitted into networks of international communication through the post and telegraph, and the hotel often supplied critical functions for these networks (King, 2016; Peleggi, 2012: 133–136). Yet Peleggi introduces a critical second dimension to the study of these places: while functioning as comfort zones in the realm of the unfamiliar for the European traveller, hotels were also 'contact zones', expressing an essential hybridity that no degree of imported management, food, or décor could extinguish. They were shaped by local environments in important ways. In comparison with the *métropole*, markedly more multi-racial populations populated colonial cities such as Colombo and Singapore. Moreover, as a marker of what Srilata Ravi (2008: 482–483) has characterised as 'patrician utopia', the colonial grand hotel offered a promontorial prospect on the unfamiliar that invited reassessments of the self. So doing, it destabilised many of the functions ascribed to the grand hotel's 'comfort zones'. The study of the colonial hotel as offering both 'comfort zones' and 'contact zones' is premised on the idea that the hotel in the colony was a fundamentally different creature from that found in the *métropole* (Peleggi, 2012: 146). There are a number of ways in which this difference was manifested and performed. Groups that may have inhabited the margins of the metropolitan grand hotel assumed relative prominence and authority in the colonial environment – in the operation of hotels, for example. The decentring of familiarity – aesthetically, for example, through the exotic embellishment of hotel exteriors and interiors – cued hotel guests that this

Figure 4.2 Shepheard's Hotel, Cairo: Moorish dining room, ca. 1860–1929

was not a home away from home, but in fact something very different indeed. And while technologically the hotel was on the vanguard of adopting familiar European services and amenities (Peleggi, 2012), restaurant cuisine could fuse the familiar and the exotic. Moreover, the racial complexion of staff was a reminder to all guests of the essential difference of the colonial hotel, one which was often embellished in the public spaces of the hotel, as the image of Shepheard's Hotel 'Moorish dining room' attests (Figure 4.2). The hotel reproduced status and racial distinctions that characterised the colonial milieu while also offering a site for co-mingling – among and between staff and guests – in ways that were often unimaginable in the *métropole*. As Anthony D. King contends, even when the colonial grand hotel's aesthetics conformed to what Peleggi (2012: 133) identifies as a common classical template, it was a site where the inflections of race and class were likely to play a far greater role in the evolution of its social and commercial regimes (King, 2016: 151). Case studies of hotels in Egypt and Asia illuminate these complex histories.

Egypt's Colonial Hotels

Egypt's hotels seemed to offer the discerning tourist comfort and contact in equal measure. Descriptions such as this 1875 account of Cairo underscore the city's disorienting, cosmopolitan character, and the marked climactic disjuncture from the *métropole*, which also invoked the hotel as a metaphor to describe the bewildering heterogeneity of the city:

At one bound I have leaped from winter into spring, and already begin to consider sunshine and soft breezes at the Nile not the exception in these Christmas times. Every thing [sic] surrounding us here is as exceptional as the climate. You ask for change of a napoleon; they give it to you in nine different currencies, Russian, Spanish, French, Italian, Turkish, English, Anglo-Indian, &c., in coins as varied as the nationalities they represent. In the hotels and in the streets you hear every known, and to you many unknown, languages spoken—the site of the Tower of Babel evidently having been in Egypt. While our pious compatriots are wending their way on Sunday to the British chapel, on flaming red posters on the walls you see announced for the entertainment of the general public on this holy day, in Italian and Arabic, a representation that is to be given by a company, 'Mimo, gymanstico-dansante, in which Chinese gymnasts assist, directed by the celebrated Bartoletti, decorated with nine medals of honour in the chief cities of Europe.' This curious blending of the Christian and the Pagan which has ever characterised Egypt is thus thrust upon you everywhere; and if there be a great hotel of nations it is here to-day, where in the course of an hour's walk you can meet the representatives of every race and hear the language of every nation under the sun save those of the Polar regions, and witness the simultaneous erection of the Mohammedan mosque and the Christian church almost side by side. ('correspondent of *Galignani's Messenger*, 31 December 1875', quoted in the *Morning Post*, 15 January 1876)

Many descriptions employed an Orientalist frame to convey the overwhelming sights, sounds and smells of the city. Sometimes they vacillated between marking the familiar and the unfamiliar, seeking imperfect reference points in the European world. Consider, within the context of this heterogeneous city, this description of Shepheard's Hotel in Cairo in the 1890s. It had become a popular winter destination for European travellers, where one writer remarked that 'visitors at the principal hotels form a society of their own':

In a sketch, then, of fashionable Cairo in the nineties, more prominence must be given to the hotels than would be necessary in most foreign watering-places. The most fashionable are, undoubtedly, the Continental, Shepheard's, and Ghezireh Palace, whose visitors' lists almost suggest a page out of the 'Almanac de Gotha.' Yet, as regards the *clientèle*, each has a distinct character of its own; and if I may attempt a somewhat invidious task, I should be inclined to say that the Continental is more peculiarly exclusive and aristocratic, while Shepheard's is smarter, and the note of modernity here is more insistent. As for the Ghezireh Palace Hotel, it is of too recent date to have acquired any distinct social characteristics. The salient features of these establishments may, perhaps, be better understood by comparison with London hotels. The Continental, then, may be compared with the Alexandra or the Albemarle, Shepheard's with the Savoy, and the Ghezireh Palace with the Cecil.

The leading hotels of Cairo can certainly compare favourably with the best hotels of the fashionable Riviera watering-places. Leaving the United States out of the question, it is, perhaps, hardly going too far to say that no extra-European city of the same size offers such a wide choice of high-class and well-appointed hotels, so well adapted to meet the demands of English travellers, as the City of the Caliphs. (Reynolds-Ball, 1897: 123)

The device of metropolitan comparison was employed here to index these places, in a description that also underlined the exceptional character of American hostelries. Shepheard's Hotel (Figure 4.3) was part of an urban hotel network in Egypt designed to the requirements of the European tourist (King, 2016: 159–160). Formerly known as the 'British Hotel', it was rechristened, relocated and reopened in 1850, receiving guests in July 1851 under the name of its owner (Humphreys, 2011: 76). It soon became Cairo's most famous hotel (Humphreys, 2011: 51).

As we have seen, historians of the hotel's aesthetics and functions have emphasised elements of hybridity and pastiche that produced curious, sometimes bewildering, chronologies and spatial configurations. Shepheard's 'Moorish dining room' illustrates this *bricolage*, but scholars have found evidence of its manifestation in many aspects of the hotel and its operation. Rajesh Heynickx (2015), exploring its lobby, has shown how even in such a comparatively controlled environment, diverse temporalities were telegraphed by historically eclectic interior décor, and by clock faces displaying a range of times. In an example of the familiar and the unfamiliar condensed in a single site, travellers found themselves surrounded by flamboyant, Orientalist decoration, yet discovered that the establishment strictly adhered to the dictates of European tea-time (Humphreys, 2011: 150–151). Aesthetic *pastiche* and regimes of sociability intersected to undermine the idea of the colonial hotel as a mere metropolitan transplant (Heynickx, 2015).

This hybridity was evident in other Egyptian hotels – such as the landmark Gezira Palace Hotel, just outside central Cairo – and signalled their complex positionings within colonised space. Employing the analytic framework of building biography, and elaborating on how the hotel can

Figure 4.3 Kairo, Shepheard's Hotel, ca. 1860–1929

be used to produce narratives of wider societies and countries and to illu-minate power relations that lie behind those narratives, Saphinaz-Amal Naguib (2008: 468) explores how the Gezira Palace Hotel developed as part of the fabric of the city. He analyses how hotel functions and aesthet-ics produced mediating spaces between local cultures and transnational tastes. Unlike many establishments explored in this survey, the Gezira Palace Hotel was not a purpose-built hotel. Indeed, it was constructed to host the French empress on instructions from the Egyptian *khedive* (Naguib, 2008: 469–470). Bankruptcy in 1879 resulted in the acquisition of the property by the Egyptian Hotels Co. Ltd in 1897, with the building thereafter adapted to a variety of purposes. It was commandeered as a British military hospital during World War I. It then served as inland water transport authority headquarters, subsequently as a private resi-dence, and then was taken over by the state after the Egyptian revolution in 1952. After 1962 it returned to its functions as a hotel (Naguib, 2008: 469–470). Aesthetically, it expressed a *mélange* of styles, with a Moorish exterior that was popular among the Egyptian middle classes in the late 19th century as they integrated within a wider culture of taste (Naguib,

2008: 477). Rather than unambiguously proclaiming metropolitan influence and imperial power, it became a stage for both the enactment of cosmopolitanism and the forging of a distinctive identity among the Egyptian middle classes. Indeed, Naguib (2008: 472) also contends that the contemporary hotel indexes the accretion of various cultural influences. It has become a site in which Egypt negotiates its postcolonial identity through the vocabulary of heritage. In exploring its instrumentality among Egyptians, rather than colonisers or tourists, he underscores the extent to which hotels served a variety of constituencies and interests, in colonial and postcolonial eras. This was true of other places, too, including Asia's grand hotels.

Colonial Hotels in Asia

Srilata Ravi (2008: 476), in her study of the Continental Hotel in Saigon in colonial and postcolonial periods, has written a building biography in which the hotel's form and aesthetics are seen as part of a broader colonial urban landscape of official and unofficial buildings that expressed planners' and administrators' efforts to tame and rationalise spaces of contact between races. The hotel was part of an effort to construct a visible, durable built environment that telegraphed 'ideals of order, cleanliness, spatial segregation and hierarchy' (Ravi, 2008: 477). Ravi remarks that hotels attempted to address colonial anxieties in various ways. Adopting a critical approach to the framing of the gaze from within the hotel, she looks carefully at its spaces to unpack the politics of their vantage-points. Emphasising the ways that a hotel's affordances structured prospects over the colonial city, Ravi contends that the Continental Hotel's terrace structured a promontory gaze over Saigon that ordered and aestheticised the urban landscape from the familiar spaces of the hotel (Ravi, 2008: 477). Following Chris Rojek's formulation of modernity, Ravi argues that the hotel was instrumental in playing out two key aspects of the modern condition: by marking the civilising ideology of colonialism on one hand, and by supplying a space for ludic and indolent behaviour on the other hand (Ravi, 2008: 480). In the postcolonial environment, such buildings have variously become derelict, been repurposed, or been materially and symbolically reconfigured as vestigial colonial institutions, reactivating 'anachronistic' features in a programme of 'colonial exotica' (Ravi, 2008: 26). The enlistment of the colonial hotel in postcolonial heritage politics is evident in Saigon, as in Cairo. Singapore's landmark hotel, Raffles, supplies a highly instructive case study of an establishment that has been enrolled within diverse historical political economies and programmes.

Perhaps no hotel better manifests the ambivalence and ambiguities of the status of grand colonial hotels in colonial and postcolonial eras than Raffles Hotel in Singapore (Figure 4.4) – an establishment whose very origins, as Ashley Jackson (2013: 181) notes, reflected eclectic influences over colonial life. It was constructed in French Renaissance style by Armenian hoteliers, the Sarkis brothers, on land acquired in 1887 by a wealthy Arab trader that housed the Beach House. The hotel, erected over the course of several decades, became a centre of the colonial system, and was later reconfigured as a symbol of Singapore's rapid postcolonial development and of Singaporean nationhood. Tracing its imperial development, King (2016: 157) notes that the diasporic background of its owners meant that Raffles was operated from a politically different stand-point than those hotels in the colonies whose ownership and management was entrusted to settlers. The latter establishments more visibly underscored the status of metropolitans as arbiters of access and underlined their authority over regimes of labour and cultures of hospitality.

Exploring Maurizio Peleggi's contention that the hotel is rarely exclusively an unambiguous inscriber of metropolitan power, in the manner, for

Figure 4.4 Singapore, exterior view of the Raffles Hotel, ca. 1941

example, of official administrative buildings (Peleggi, 2012: 126), Daniel P.S. Goh (2010) traces Raffles Hotel's positioning within three distinct sets of overarching political and economic structures. He identifies them as: (1) British colonialism; (2) postcolonial capitalism; and (3) neoliberal globalisation. So doing, he skilfully demonstrates what the hotel reveals about the character and culture of these stages of 'transnational capitalism', and about Singapore's position within them. In charting this trajectory, Goh identifies discrete phases to which the hotel's functions were adapted, and in which its regimes of space and sociality, power and time evolved. In the colonial period, as Singapore became a critical entrepôt, the hotel signified domestic comfort and refuge from imperial capitalist networks. In the colonial phase, Goh argues that the spaces of the pastiche French Renaissance edifice (erected to replace the original bungalow-style building in 1897) were sites of familiarity for a colonial elite who participated in the era's colonial capitalist networks (Goh, 2010: 180).

What distinguishes Goh's scholarship from other work on colonial hotels is that the colonial period serves as a starting point for the analysis of institutional transformation – 'transfiguration' in his terminology – through postcolonial conditions. After independence, during the brief period in which Singapore was integrated within the Malayan federation, the hotel itself, while under Chinese ownership, was adapted to the political exigencies of 'Malayanisation', as it responded to the ideological priorities of the 'developmental state'. At the same time, it continued to reproduce the trappings of middle-class colonialism for those travellers who sought it out as a site of Oriental wonder (Goh, 2010: 183). In its final stages, enacted under the conditions of the independent Singaporean city-state, Raffles Hotel has become an object of nostalgic commodification and national monument-making through programmes of restoration. These programmes align it with the efforts of a sovereign state to capitalise on heritage by activating affective dispositions towards the building and by marketing it as a world-class hotel to an elite, cosmopolitan and globalised clientele. The charged debate surrounding this programme has implicated the government, architects, the public and urban planners over the adoption of a colonial aesthetic – 'restoring' the building to 1915 – and in particular the visibility of a new, colonial-style portico which explicitly referenced the establishment's European roots (Goh, 2010: 186–187). The hotel has been transfigured into a monument to historical European elitism, through which it now participates in the logic of contemporary global capitalism. Goh insists that the capacities for the hotel to serve as a monument to capital are as insidious as they are persistent. The hotel is able to transfigure according to new logics attached to the evolving scales and structures of capitalism. In seeking to clarify the modalities through which those changes occur by charting the hotel's historical physical and symbolic adaptations to the logic of colonial capitalism, through postcolonialism and a globalised neoliberal order, he demonstrates ways in which the hotel expressed protean relations of social, economic and political power and the conditions of colonial and postcolonial modernity.

Focusing more closely on the question of the hotel's embroilment in the contemporary politics of heritage which Goh also explores, Joan C. Henderson (2001) argues that Raffles Hotel has become part of a repertoire of cultural symbols that challenges the hegemony of colonialism and instead expresses the motivations of the postcolonial state to harness monuments to its own ends through ideologies of heritage conservation. While decolonised states often face dilemmas surrounding the appropriate use and preservation of buildings that signified the power of the colonial system, these meanings and associations are not necessarily fixed. Perhaps unsurprisingly, a hotel associated so closely with colonialism, and indeed christened after Singapore's British 'founder', Sir Stamford Raffles, has occupied an ambiguous place in the state's efforts to reconfigure the meaning of, and maximise the monetary value from, surviving colonial institutions. Maurizio Peleggi (2005) has also explored the processes through which Raffles and other colonial hotels are materially and discursively reconfigured within a framework that aims to cement their status as historic landmarks, with reference to colonial attributes and narratives that seem at odds with their political environments. Colonial associations offer the potential to draw tourists, given the fame that accrued to the establishment through the writing of Somerset Maugham and others. In consequence, the 'European' dimension of the hotel's narrative, represented in the 'restoration' of its 1915 aesthetic, is heavily favoured over Asian elements. Henderson (2001: 24) suggests that rather than reproducing subservience to the narrative of colonialism, the heritage project can be viewed as part of an effort by sovereign states to carve out autonomous identities and also develop a lucrative trade within the context of a competitive global tourist economy.

The Postcolonial Hotel

The work of Goh, Henderson, Peleggi and others demonstrate how hotels' material forms and symbolisms vary widely from colonial periods to the present day, and are highly dependent on the local contexts of colonialism and decolonisation. This is affirmed by other case studies. Some buildings, such as Watson's Esplanade Hotel in Bombay, have been repurposed. Their original status, stature and functions are obscured in the contemporary urban landscape, rendering their colonial associations relatively illegible. Some establishments, such as Shepheard's Hotel in Cairo, have been razed. Others, such as Raffles Hotel, have been discursively repositioned and materially altered, under programmes of 'preservation', to serve the agenda of the postcolonial state and current dominant economic interests.

Hotels erected under periods of colonial control need not signify the authority of the colonising power. Under colonial regimes, and in certain contexts, for example, hotels can have the potential to express incipient nationalism. In Israel, where the colonial project involved a European state, Britain, overseeing a place of increasing European settlement, for example, a distinctive hotel design found embryonic form in the era of the British Palestinian mandate, when a modernist aesthetic – later strongly associated with post-Independence Israel – was forged by European architects, fusing what Daniella Ohad Smith has described as 'a real need for modern architecture, futuristic aesthetics, and utopian national aspirations' (Smith, 2010: 99). She 'reads' the hotel in the British mandatory period as expressing the close relationship between 'hotel design and political and national aspirations' (Smith, 2010: 99), integrating European diasporic interests in the construction of a coherent Utopian design. Smith identifies the stark, largely unornamented style as heralding a break from the conventional colonial aesthetic and an embrace of a template for hotel design that reflected the tenets of Zionism: progress, youthfulness and modernity. It offered a tool in the symbolic and material construction of a Zionist landscape, epitomised by the Eden Hotel. In this case, the hotel is seen as materialising ideological precepts that were foundational to Israeli national identity, projecting them in built form *before* the political state was built. Its history underlines how the hotel form, under certain circumstances, can anticipate, rather than follow, political independence.

Hotels in European settler societies outside the United States of America also illuminate ways colonial and postcolonial identities and networks are negotiated through the built form. In places such as Australia and Canada, for example, the hotel was implicated in integrating the nation symbolically and materially within the colonial system. The networks of metropolitan capital that often realised it, and the form of the grand hotel itself, reflected these influences. In Canada, Rhodri Windsor Liscombe (1993) has shown that the grand hotel assumed a distinctive architectural form that synthesised French Second Empire and Scottish baronial influences to produce a distinctive built form. Indeed, the

Figure 4.5 Hotel Frontenac, Dufferin Terrace, Quebec City, QC, 1900

château style epitomised by Quebec City's Château Frontenac (Figure 4.5) was appropriated as a national style – the iconic form of the Canadian grand hotel that was associated with the railway hotel in particular (Chisholm *et al.*, 2001; Kalman, 1968). It had political salience as an aesthetic that married the influences (and thereby signified the narrative) of the nation's two putative 'founding peoples' – French and British. It gained currency as the *château* style declined in popularity in both the US and the UK, and was naturalised as a distinctive Canadian style (Liscombe, 1993: 135).

In colonial urban Australia, specific local influences, notably economic conditions, spurred the development of distinctive forms of commercial accommodation, resulting in a hesitant, but discernible movement from poorly built shanties in colonial Victoria to more capital-intensive, large-scale hotels (O'Mahony & Clark, 2013). Examining Sydney's landmark hotel 'The Australia' from the perspective of building biography, Donald McNeill and Kim McNamara (2012) situate the hotel's 'life' within a late 19th- and early 20th-century urban network in which leading establishments were adaptors of technologies, boasting sophisticated communication systems and playing a critical role in the evolution of urban geographies and economies with strong links to the British imperial world. The hotel's fate was determined, in their analysis, in part by the decline of the global imperial network of which it was a part, as much as any of the hotels of colonial-era Asia or Africa. Imperialism and postcolonialism are critical frameworks within which to understand the diverse 'life-courses' of such hotels in colonial and postcolonial settings, and to evaluate their divergent paths and enrolments within postcolonial political, economic and cultural programmes.

Conclusion

Scholarship on the relationship between tourism and postcolonial societies has grappled with whether the act of tourism reproduces and sustains, to some degree, elements of colonialism, and whether the practices, infrastructures and institutions of tourism reconstitute the colonial system, both materially (through the retrenchment of economic imbalances, for example), and symbolically (through the reification of colonial-era objects and relations in the development of the tourism product) (Hall & Tucker, 2004). The historical analysis of hotels clarifies these relationships in diverse colonial environments. Hotels in postcolonial environments have been handled in strikingly different ways. In Cairo, the city's famous Shepheard's Hotel was framed in the discourses of anti-colonialism as a site of anachronistic, even toxic, symbolisms associated with a disparaged external power. Its malignant meanings were inscribed so deeply in the urban landscapes that advocates of a postcolonial political order felt compelled to obliterate it, as the next chapter discusses. Indeed, in the post-1952 revolutionary period in Egypt, new architectural styles were adopted to symbolise a break from the colonial period – even if they carried a foreign name. Annabel Wharton contends that the new post-World War II Hilton hotel inscribed freedom from colonial systems of authority (Wharton, 2001: 2). Yet Singapore's Raffles Hotel was not subject to destruction, replacement, or repurposing, but rather to 'decommissioning' and symbolic and material reconfiguring, following the priorities of a heritage programme sponsored by a sovereign state and guided by specific political priorities and economic incentives (du Cros, 2004: 164).

In the postcolonial era, many hotels have also been central to contested political programmes by which the colonial era is reimagined and materialised for tourist consumption. The enclavic Mauritius Sugar Beach Resort hotel, for example (Kothari, 2015: 249), is a highly managed space that evokes similar resorts throughout the world – places characterised by a more fixed physical barrier than the grand urban hotel, and that exist outside the more heterogeneous tourist spaces. Such hotels and resorts are often places in which the 'outside' world is carefully choreographed and displayed as a form of controlled 'edutainment' within resort walls. In addition to performing otherness in ways that reproduce topographical and cultural imaginaries and resonate with entrenched ideas about the colonial era, reinforcing such themes as tropicality, which are also produced and reproduced in Caribbean sites, these places are often materially networked within economies of tourism and hospitality that reproduce colonial relationships – such as the export of tourism sector profits from the locality to a metropolitan centre (Kothari, 2015: 251). This interpretation of the enclavic resort is premised on the postcolonial tourist site being bound in a system which effectively materially and culturally replicates binary colonial spatial regimes and social relations. Uma Kothari, however, argues that there are ways in which the dominance of the colonist framework is subverted, manipulated and exploited to the advantage of previously subordinated, marginalised and colonised populations. Moreover, the consumption of themed space admits of many 'interspatial reference points' which, as Tim Edensor and Kothari remark, undermine their 'coherence as illusory bound spaces' (Edensor & Kothari, 2004: 198). The history of colonial-era hotels offers diverse examples to support such claims, underlining the protean identities of the hotel during and after colonialism. Moreover, the 'colonial hotel' exists as an imaginative construct, with powerful connotations, though the hotels ranged widely in form throughout areas under European authority. Still, hotels have historically been susceptible to identification as markers of 'external' authority. Indeed, this is one of several ways that hotels have become implicated in systems of violence – the focus of the next chapter.

5 The Wartime Hotel

Many parties in places of violent conflict identify hotels as sites of great strategic value. Hotels have been among the visible participants in landscapes of urban war and violence, from Lebanon's Battle of the Hotels in the 1970s, to the Irish Republican Army's bombing of the Conservative Party conference at the Grand Hotel in 1984, to the urban sieges of the Balkan conflicts of the 1990s, to the Canal Hotel bombing in Baghdad in 2003, which targeted the United Nations Assistance Mission in Iraq. Their entanglements in recent conflicts have highlighted hotels' diverse functions, symbolisms and vulnerabilities. This is not a new phenomenon. Hotels have long been commandeered and used in times of war – for quartering combatants, for example. War has re-shaped hotel markets and workforces, often in dramatic ways, such as the expulsion of 'enemy aliens' from the labour force, and the (often temporary) replacement by females of male workers who were sent to the front. Hotels have been associated with hostile actors and ideologies, and as such become targets. The conventional history of the hotel-as-target identifies the bombing of the King David Hotel, the UK's mandatory headquarters, by the Jewish underground Irgun movement in 1946 as the first such attack in modern times (Paraskevas, 2013: 141; Wernick & Von Gillow, 2012: 736). In 1948 the Semiramis Hotel suffered a similar fate at the hands of Haganah, who identified it as a site housing local Arab militiamen. The hotel has assumed specific tactical and symbolic salience in the context of modern terrorism and urban guerrilla warfare. Modern colonialism and American political and economic hegemony – discussed in preceding chapters as contexts in which the meaning of hotels have developed – have become especially salient to understanding hotels' symbolisms and their historical enrolment within conflicts.

Take the case of Egypt, whose sector was greatly impacted by the outbreak of World War I in 1914. Many Egyptian hotels were used by soldiers (Lyth, 2013: 187), requisitioned by the Army and adapted as hospitals (Humphreys, 2011: 68). *Caterer, Hotel Keeper, and Restaurateurs' Gazette* reported on 15 February 1915 that '[t]he Teuton visitor is, of course, entirely barred, Americans have been kept at home by the crisis, and so have the British and French visitors', resulting in the closure of many of the country's hotels. Quoting *The Times*, it noted that a few establishments remained open, among them the Grand Continental and Shepheard's Hotel. In contrast, the Savoy, Semiramis and Gezira Hotels had shuttered (*Caterer, Hotel Keeper, and Restaurateurs' Gazette*, 15 February 1915, 55). Yet there was also life in the hotel trade: Cairo had 'become militarised', and Shepheard's Hotel and the Grand Continental Hotel 'swarm[ed] with officers of every rank and every branch in the Imperial Service'. In place of the tourists at the Mena House, Australian military personnel camped near the pyramids. German and Austrian waiters had vacated their positions, but Egyptians and Berbers took their place.

Such disruptions, reuses and reallocations of resources in hotels during conflicts reveal how the hotels' customary markets were imperilled, and also how hotels were enlisted within the war effort, supplying sites for soldiers' camps, strategic nerve-centres, spaces of sociability, and storage depots for supplies. Contrast these circumstances with the position of Shepheard's Hotel four decades later, when it was embroiled in fierce conflict nourished by Arab nationalism and focused on symbols of European colonialism. On 9 February 1952, *The Illustrated London News* featured vivid photographs of nationalist riots that had gripped Cairo in response to the British seizure of the police barracks in Ismailia (Figure 5.1). British businesses, including the offices of Thomas Cook and Son, were set upon, damaged and destroyed: 'The famous Shepheard's Hotel was attacked, set on fire and left a mere pile of ruins' (*The Illustrated London News*, 9 February 1952, 204). Underneath the image of a crumbling pile was a caption: 'All that remains of one of the world's most famous hotels: Shepheard's Hotel, after the ferocious twelve-hour-long rioting of 26 January, in which British residents were murdered by the mob' (*The Illustrated London News*, 9 February 1952, 205).

How can we understand how Egypt's most famous hotel became an object of the mob's ire? Britain remained the European hegemon in Egypt after the 1882 invasion to defend its extensive financial interest in the country, until 1952, when King Farouk, who was sympathetic to British interests, was overthrown in a revolution that brought Arab nationalist Gamal Abdel Nasser to power. To some participants in the 1952 revolution, Shepheard's Hotel signified the longstanding imposition of authority by an external power that they rejected – the building's physical conquest and destruction were integral to the symbolic repudiation of the colonial project and its toxic legacy.

A biography of Shepheard's Hotel invites reflection on how hotels historically have been entangled in conflicts. In considering this question, often the politically inscribed meaning of the place refer to its history, and

Figure 5.1 Shepheard's Hotel in ruins, 1952

to the actors who financed it, its markets and functions within the context of formal or informal colonialism, and how it evolved as a legible marker of relations of political, cultural and economic power. This is especially true when modern conflicts see hotels associated with Western political power, Western-backed regimes, Western capital and urban topographies that developed in the colonial era. There are critical contexts to this discussion of hotels and violence discussed in the chapter that follows: the first relates to hotels as targets of terrorist violence, and the second to hotels in zones of conflict between more formal belligerents. Both underline the ways in which hotels have become embroiled in violence.

Openness, Vulnerability and Securitisation

Hotels have often been explored as sites of sporadic violence – including suicide and homicide. The assassinations of Martin Luther King Jr in the Lorraine Motel in Memphis and Robert F. Kennedy in the Ambassador Hotel in Los Angeles, both in 1968, as well as many assassinations by terrorist groups and intelligence agencies, supply moments in the annals of hotel history in which the hotel's historically defining roles supplying shelter and safety are dramatically undermined. Recent, high-profile cases of armed assaults on places of commercial accommodation, from Kabul, to Mumbai, to Amman, to Mombasa and Jakarta, have underscored the vulnerability of the hotel to attack, and have attracted scholars concerned with questions of securitisation and terrorist strategy (Wernick & Von Gillow, 2012), as have historical cases in which hotels are selected as targets not because of the presence of any hostile person or group dwelling within them, but rather because of their general association with a particular clientele, such as an external agency, a non-governmental organisation, or a sovereign power. Aspects of the hotel's physical form – its intrinsic openness, for example, and success in framing it as a 'foreign entity', can make it a target for groups seeking to undermine the legitimacy of civil authority, heighten public fear and boldly demonstrate their capabilities in unconventional forms of combat, when other resources are asymmetrically distributed.

Historical studies of hotels in wartime draw heavily on contemporary social science, and especially security and strategic studies, in developing a framework for understanding such events. In such scholarship, a number of features of hotels have been identified as critical in shaping their relative value as targets – some relate to symbolisms, which can link them to a perceived hostile or foreign adversary or ideology, and others to material characteristics, such as comparatively low levels of securitisation, and the value of their spaces to belligerents in the prosecution of war.

The hotel falls along a continuum of places that are generally considered 'soft targets'. Hotels are comparatively open spaces: indeed, they proclaim, in fulfilling their core business function as sites of hospitality, to be accessible to strangers. Their efficient and profitable operation relies upon a high level of accessibility (although this can be severely reduced in times of war). Hotels are not just open for human circulation: the spread of Severe Acute Respiratory Syndrome, Legionnaires' Disease and other malignancies through the spaces of hotels reveals their intrinsic permeability. Their use-values to parties in other crises, such as natural disasters, also means that they are conscripted in times of emergency. Figure 5.2 shows a downtown Louisville, Kentucky hotel that was repurposed as a flood relief station: missing persons reports were completed and telecommunications systems were devoted to the aftermath of the natural disaster. The potential for hotels to supply shelter from surrounding, violent

Figure 5.2 Flood relief station at Louisville Hotel, Louisville, Kentucky, 1937

upheaval has also been underscored by the story of the Hôtel des Mille Collines in Kigali, Rwanda, where over a thousand people sought refuge in 1994, when the country descended into brutal, fratricidal conflict. The functions of the hotel as a place of involuntary inhabitation are underscored in conflicts, when refugees are often housed in them in other states. This conceptualisation of the hotel as a site of coercive inhabitation in wartime (and in peacetime) demands greater attention.

Because of their historical roles supplying shelter or sanctuary – an important and foundational characteristic of hotels – hotels can also be subject to violent attack. Individuals or groups may wish to acquire control of the building to shelter there themselves, or they may target a hotel because the population being sheltered there is regarded as hostile. On other occasions, the prominence of the hotel may contribute to the spectacularisation of violence, which achieves a number of goals for perpetrators. As soft targets, hotels join a host of sites that includes shopping malls, mass transport systems, schools and churches. As Brian T. Bennett (2007: 62) notes, the very purpose of a soft target is served by a high degree of permeability, characterised by a belligerent's 'relatively unimpeded access to large concentrations of people'. Levels of securitisation vary by institution and context. Those establishments that command greater resources, host potentially sensitive actors, occupy more vulnerable locations, and carry potentially high symbolic value are often subject to a higher degree of securitisation through barriers which restrict public access (Lisle, 2013). Scholars, following the theoretical model outlined by Michel Foucault, have been interested in the ways in which hotels serve as loci for exploring biopolitics – not just investigating regimes that survey and seek to control human lives, but the wider systems of technology and information in which they are implicated (Lisle, 2013). These systems are not merely activated in wartime – as we have seen, from the hotel detective, to systems of manual registration, hotel surveillance has historically been enacted in a variety of manners in peacetime, too, despite the putative licence and freedoms associated with hotel space. Hotel spaces, which are not generally designed to engender a heightened sense of vulnerability, and often supress visible systems of surveillance, can predispose people to reduced awareness of threats (Henderson *et al.*, 2010). Wartime, though, often dramatically underscores systems and mechanisms of scrutiny.

Following the logic of the belligerent, the propagandistic value of targeting hotels can be heightened if hotels can be presented as an unambiguously hostile site – one associated closely with an adversary – whether a state, a foreign entity or power, or a social, cultural, or economic interest that is perceived as antagonistic. Their destruction can simultaneously devastate critical infrastructures, attract significant media attention and induce civil destabilisation and social insecurity, while belligerents enhance their prestige and profile. But hotels can also be targets of second resort, when asymmetrical resources, internal weaknesses, or enhanced security make assaults on other sites, such as military installations, much more difficult (Wernick & Von Gillow, 2012: 735–736).

In exploring the strategic contexts in which the hotel historically has been framed as a legitimate target of violence, it is useful to enumerate material and symbolic features that have made it susceptible to violent attack. According to the logic of perpetrators of violence against a hotel, their value as targets is enhanced:

(1) by servicing a clientele that is socially, culturally, economically and/or politically dissimilar from the belligerents and their base, thereby reducing positive affective attachment to the site and losses of life connected to an attack on it among the supporters of the perpetrator, and perhaps the wider population (though the act of attacking an hotel can frequently draw in workers, bystanders and others not connected to either the targeted population or even to the institution itself);

(2) by evoking 'strong psychological and emotional reactions' (Martin, 2010: 366) through the hotel's links to actors that can be cast as hostile to the belligerents and their base. These may include hotels with links to foreign (often Western) hotel brands, or hotels that have abiding historical, iconic associations with contested systems of political control;

(3) by functioning in ways that can symbolically or materially degrade the capacities of a targeted group – such as instances when hotels serve as sites of administrative control over a territory by a state or party whose legitimacy the belligerents reject, or when hotels host infrastructures that are regarded as part of a hostile apparatus; and

(4) by offering strategic advantages to the belligerents, in part through their open nature, facilitating reconnaissance ahead of the operation (Wernick & Von Gillow, 2012: 735). In some cases, the repurposing and/or high securitisation of hotels, behind fortified zones, has de-territorialised hotels and, in seeming to remove them from their 'host' environments, enhanced their prestige value as symbols of otherness and domination. In this sense they can be cast as being part of the infrastructure of illegitimate authority.

While a number of these characteristics proceed from the hotel's status as an intrinsically open place, it is also an institution with profound inscriptional power and potentially potent symbolisms, especially when associated with Western modernity – two themes that have been explored in earlier discussions on American and colonial hotels. In many cases, the imperative of its conquest and/or destruction is seen as integral to the programmatic effort at civil destabilisation, engendering wider anxiety, shoring up support for an organisation and ideology, undermining civil authority and producing a narrative of 'liberation' from external dominance.

Wartime Hotels

Previous chapters have explored narratives of American and colonial hotel development, and underscored how, despite the wide range of forms and contexts in which establishments of commercial accommodation operated in the US and in diverse European colonies, scholars have tended to ascribe shared features and a single institutional form to the 'American hotel' and the 'colonial hotel'. It has also examined how the forms and meanings of hotels have changed over time. What happens when the very stability of the environment in which a hotel's identity was erected – and which it helps to order – is threatened by war? We can learn a great deal about its identity and representations of the hotel in wartime by surveying the growing critical literature that connects the hotel to fragile and failing urban systems, technologies of destruction and to its status as a site of refuge, as a strategic asset in wartime and as a space which becomes central to enacting transitions from conflict to peace. The historical case studies are largely drawn from the recent past, partly because of the distinctive character of irregular urban combat in the 20th century – and underline the value of adopting a longer chronology to explore the involvement of hotels in conflict. Assessing the geopolitical significance of the hotel allows us to reassess the nostalgic narrative expressed by Michel de Grèce (1987), whose paean to Beirut's Saint-Georges Hotel expressed longing for the certainties of the colonial era. Observing the ravages that civil conflict had visited upon the landmark hostelry constructed in the interwar period, when Lebanon was under a French mandate, and when it was strongly associated with a glamorous, cosmopolitan narrative of urban life, Grèce lamented that Lebanon's brutal war had effaced the hotel's essential functions and meanings:

> Many a haven has been obliterated by politics. What remains of the *Saint-Georges* in Beirut? If this great institution is ever rebuilt on its rock by the sea will it ever recapture the atmosphere that made it so utterly unique? In the mellow bar of the *Saint-Georges*, journalists, politicians, dealers, millionaires, informers, courtesans and other celebrities from all over the Middle East were wont to gather. The place epitomised that special ambience of worldliness, frivolity and excitement which used to be the Lebanon.

Beirut at the time of Michel de Grèce's lamentation had descended into a fratricidal conflict. The urban landscape was engulfed by violence in which hotels were key 'victims' but also sites of fierce contest. The Saint-Georges Hotel's bar, eulogised by Saïd K. Aburish in 1989 as the epicentre of a local, regional and national information network over many years, was decommissioned.

The Saint-Georges' experience was an example of hotels' embroilment in 20th-century civil conflicts that other historians have chronicled and dissected. Robert A. Davidson (2018), for example, illuminates the contested meanings associated with a hotel as it becomes subsumed in civil conflict. Using the example of the Hotel Colon in Barcelona during Spain's Civil War, Davidson explores how the vantage-points of the hotel, once commodified in the context of leisure and other peacetime purposes, assumed a radical new, and prized, value as a tactical 'sightline'. Moreover, in Barcelona, where the weakness of the central state led a range of parties to seize public buildings, Davidson argues that the hotel played a critical role mediating between the global and the local – an extension of a role it had assumed in an earlier, peacetime period when it had been a critical mediator of Barcelona's and Catalonia's encounter with liberalism and capitalism. No longer conduits for such political and economic ideologies, or for cultural movements such as the Jazz Age, Barcelona's grand hotels, under the control of International Socialists and anarcho-syndicalists, channelled strikingly different political ideals.

Some wartime hotels have been completely repurposed for combat, as Danny Hoffman observes in his study of Brookfields Hotel in Freetown, Sierra Leone. There, hotels during the brutal civil conflict of the late 20th and early 21st century ceased to become permeable places of hospitality and operated more as citadels – or barracks (Hoffman, 2005, 2007). In the process, Hoffman contends that when government-sponsored militias moved into, and fortified, Brooksfields Hotel during a period of intense tumult, they reconfigured the hotel's spaces 'of pleasure and profit' (Hoffman, 2005: 57). Its swimming pool was adapted as a football pitch and its balconies supplied strategically important vantage-points, even as it, paradoxically, continued to host a hotel and tourism training centre on its grounds. In contrast to these reconfigurations of the basic functions of the establishments, hotels can also serve as eerie oases of comparative safety and normalcy in a city engulfed by war – servicing the requirements of the international press, the international diplomatic community and others. As enclavic spaces, unrelenting violence seems to be suspended at their doors.

There is a way of conceiving of the functions of hotels during conflicts that reconciles the tensions between their experiences of apparent isolation from, and integral positions within, many conflict zones: as *mediators* through which the prosecution, interpretation, communication and even the resolution of conflict is shaped. Recently, Sara Fregonese and Adam Ramadan (2015) have developed a research agenda that identifies the hotel as an active shaper of the contours of war and peace. They identify six broad roles assigned to hotels, and, so doing, offer valuable tools to the historian:

(1) the hotel as a projector of soft power, a feature which structures both its physical form and its symbolic value;
(2) the hotel as a soft target of violence, owing to its positioning as an institution which, however fortified, still maintains some greater degree of 'openness';
(3) the hotel as a strategic infrastructure, often related to its location and resources;

(4) the hotel as a site for war reporting;
(5) the hotel as a site supplying hospitality or care, sometimes when it is requisitioned and repurposed as a hospital or convalescent institution (the hotel can also supply spaces that function as a morgue); and
(6) the hotel as an institution of peace building.

With regards to this last function, hotels' symbolisms and spaces can sometimes make them amenable to framing as 'neutral ground' for resolution of conflicts, as when the historic Mena House Hotel served as a site for peace negotiations between Egypt and Israel in 1977. John K. Walton (2012: 13) underlines this point, arguing for the systematic, critical study of the role of the international and transnational history of the resort as a site of diplomatic activity, incidents and even scandal.

The use-value of a hotel to various actors in conflict zones, including the press and neutral parties, is measured through a calculation that encompasses people it houses (workers and guests), its location, its spaces, and the materials it stores. In wartime, the hotel can be mobilised materially and symbolically in new ways, sometimes as prosaically as producing new demand for its conventional roles supplying lodging, entertainment and nourishment. In World War I, for example, American domestic tourism increased and supplied a growing market for hotels, even as the number of overseas visitors fell (Hayner, 1936: 135). This was common in wartime, during which demand for some hotel services and amenities – such as restaurant meals and alcohol – were diminished by restrictions introduced by the state, even as demand rose for other hotel goods, spaces and services.

As Lisa Fregonese and Adam Ramadan underline, hotels play a critical role in *shaping* violent conflict. We might not agree with Lisa Smirl that 'every conflict has its hotel' (Smirl, 2016: 32) – sometimes no single establishment achieves the iconic status of the Holiday Inn during the siege of Sarajevo, or the Saint-Georges Hotel in Beirut's vicious violence. But in conflict zones the basic functions of the hotel can often persist, though not always in ways that its designers, managers, staff and peacetime clientele intended or imagined. The civil strife which engulfed Beirut in the 1970s and Sarajevo in the 1990s offer backdrops for exploring the strategic realignment of urban hotels according to new values ascribed to their physical affordances and their symbolisms.

Beirut's Battle of the Hotels

In Beirut's so-called Battle of the Hotels during the Lebanese Civil War, buildings became assets to various warring militias. They were also crucial to defining the line that divided hostile combatants, and to shaping the structure of urban warfare and public consciousness of the conflict. Sara Fregonese has developed an ambitious agenda for the study of the hotel focusing on Beirut's period of 'urbicide' from the mid-1970s to the early 1990s (Fregonese, 2009; Graham, 2004). Her approach emphasises how an establishment's history was framed in ways that freighted it symbolically and made it vulnerable to conquest and/or demolition as part of the logic of the conflict. Inscriptions of colonial power are central to these representations. Fregonese traces the descent of the city into fratricidal war through the prism of its iconic hotels, seeing them in part as markers of the cosmopolitanism inscribed in specific institutions and neighbourhoods over the preceding century. Instead of charting what she sees as the eclipse of a civic openness in the city through wartime retrenchment, she observes a dialectic playing out in hotel space, as elsewhere with the urban fabric. Fregonese hones in on a longitudinal analysis of Beirut's seaside district, and the identities ascribed to it as a distinctive place apart from the fabric of the wider city. Critically, Fregonese's analysis of the political economy of the conflict traces the origins of the discourse within which the city is embedded – fragilely balanced between its status as a refuge and a battleground – to governmentalities developed under the 19th-century *colonial system*. In zeroing in on the functions and symbolisms of the city's hotels, she identifies technologies of communications that dwelled within them as a critical infrastructure that proclaimed the openness of Beirut's economy and its embeddedness within transnational capitalism in the 1960s (2012: 322–323). In so doing, she identifies both colonialism and postcolonial capitalism as contexts which are critical to understand the de-territorialisation of the hotels and the city's hotel district and their consequent susceptibility to enlistment within the conflict as valued sites of conquest.

Prominent hostelries were central to the discourses of Beirut's vaunted cosmopolitanism, but also were sites for the production and reproduction of socio-economic inequalities (Fregonese, 2012: 318). The Phoenicia Hotel, opened in 1961, was part of a host of luxury hotels that erected a micro-culture of inter-related technological, communication and commercial amenities which contrasted with resources outside the district, and within Beirut more generally (Fregonese, 2012: 322–323). They constituted what Fregonese calls an 'infrastructure of hospitality' that networked the district with other global urban centres. Financed by Western capital, but staffed primarily by local workers, the district inculcated a distinctive set of social relations through the ubiquity and influence of its hotels, marked by precarious and marginal relations between workers and its cosmopolitan hotel culture, nourishing a culture of alienation (Fregonese, 2012: 324). This history of the establishments and the district in which they were located had direct bearing on their status during the civil war. With strengthening sectarian tensions and the outbreak of violence in 1975, the city centre hotel district, with its proximity to the improvised 'Green Line' that divided belligerents, and the strategic value of its buildings, became the site of intensified fighting. The famous Beirut Holiday Inn (Figure 5.3) fell to militias in March 1976 (Fregonese, 2012: 325), signalling its engulfment in the conflict.

The 'fall' of these urban hotels not only signified the appropriation of institutions for purposes of prosecuting conflict. It also extinguished their signification as markers of cosmopolitanism and processes of de-territorialisation, and 'returned' them to spaces that surrounded them, from which they had long stood apart. Foreign nationals and businesses fled the city. The seizure of the hotels and their incorporation within the infrastructure of combat articulated a symbolic conquest of key signifiers of Western capital and modernity. The collapse of the hotel sector as a marker of Western-financed, precariously mediated cosmopolitanism as it became part of the logic of the conflict – in both its physical and symbolic manifestations – made the hotel district central to the unfolding narrative of Beirut's urbicide, and underlined its centrality in shaping a narrative of the wider war (Boano & Chabarek, 2013; Fregonese, 2009).

Figure 5.3 Beirut Holiday Inn, 2007

This analysis offers a compelling case for understanding the hotels' roles in violent conflicts in relation to their historical (sometimes colonialist) associations and paths of development, as well as the identities that are erected when they themselves are built in bricks and mortar, concrete and steel. The 1990s Balkan Wars offer another stark example of the tensions between the hotel, the spaces it inhabited, and the meanings ascribed to hotels as barometers of urban stability and prosperity.

Hotels in the Siege of Sarajevo

When hotels are commandeered or seized as trophies of war, when they are requisitioned, when they are bombarded, when they house journalists as 'press hotels' (Morrison, 2016: 34), and supply access to communications technologies and other assets that are in short supply elsewhere, their carefully stewarded brand can be deeply affected. In places where they are surrounded by violent conflict, their strategic role is different, and is often in stark relief. Customary operations and markets are superseded by urgent new roles and new inhabitants. Often they are subject to more coercive, external management, and occasionally to physical destruction. The symbolisms of the wartime hotel can be striking – not just when they are damaged, laid to waste, or remain incongruously intact amidst the devastations of war. The unrehabilitated, postwar, bombed-out hotel can serve as a landmark in the urban landscape, a testament to an historical period of 'urbicide', while its renovation can be a potent signal of urban recovery and the return to normalcy.

Lisa Smirl (2016) has charted the experience of the Holiday Inn Sarajevo, as the city entered into a period of violence during the collapse of the Yugoslav state. She explores ways in which the progress of the siege, and the narrative of 'besiegement', were shaped by the material affordances of the hotel, the differential mobilities of its inhabitants, the communicative capacities that are produced by its physical location within the city and its own internal spatial regime, and the role that its technologies played in relaying the 'story' of the war to the wider public. Smirl contends that the establishment did not simply supply accommodation and amenities for the many members of the press who were based there during the long siege of 1992–6. Rather, forms and degrees of access to the hotel produced differential mobilities and relationships to the surrounding conflict – the comparative ability of guests to come to, and leave, the city contrasted with the position of residents who were, for the most part, rendered immobile within the warzone. Hotel employees in such situations inhabited a grey zone, enclosed in the spaces of the hotel, but also tethered to the city, whose landscapes they were usually compelled to navigate as inhabitants and as workers. The hotel's access to resources, often though black and grey market channels, also differentiated its denizens' privileges and their status from those of residents outside its walls. And its spatial configuration had profound implications for how the conflict was reported. Smirl's study shows the extent to which hotel resources and spatialities in a heavily mediated environment shaped social solidarities, identities and narratives of war, which tended to reflect the echo-chamber of the enclavic space and the specific vantagepoints that the hotel afforded onto the conflict. This is a point elaborated by Robert A. Davidson (2018) with piercing insight as he explores European hotels in World War II as 'journalists' space': the lobby bars of leading hotels such as the Savoy in London became 'clearinghouses' for war information. As the 20th century progressed, Davidson argues that hotel spaces became ever more crucial to the shaping and relaying of war narratives, along the lines that Lisa Smirl identifies in Sarajevo. Smirl elaborates on the ways in which a 'scopic regime' was forged through the physical affordances of the hotel – a point Davidson (2018) expounds with clarity, and one which had profound impacts on how the conflict and the urban landscape of war were narrated and communicated to the wider world through diverse media.

Kenneth Morrison (2016) expertly dissects the geography of hotel spaces and their uses as the former Yugoslavia frayed and fell apart – the Grand Hotel in Pristina, and the Hyatt and Intercontinental Hotels in Belgrade supplying spaces for interactions between journalists, politicians and combatants (Morrison, 2016: 42–43). His analysis ranks as one of the most rigorous surveys that illuminates the dynamics of war (and peace) as they played out in the confines of hotels, and charts the protean systems of signification in which the hotel was enrolled – as a beacon of Olympic idealism, Yugoslavia's comparative openness to Western capitalism, and civil disruption and cataclysm.

The history of the Holiday Inn Sarajevo, which was built to mark the 1984 Winter Olympics but went on to play a critical role in the protracted civil conflict in that city in the 1990s, traces the descent of the Olympic city into ruins. The research agenda proposed by Sara Fregonese and Adam Ramadan (2015) was outlined earlier in this chapter. It offers a number of discrete functions through which the hotel, as a built form and as part of a symbolic landscape, can influence the shape of war and peace. The symbolism of a hotel can change as markedly in war, as the transformation of the Holiday Inn Sarajevo reveals. It began as a beacon of Olympic ideals, through which Yugoslavia laid claim to a place among nations and asserted its status as a non-aligned Balkan state with a suit-able modern infrastructure that knitted the hostelry within a network of roads and venues (Morrison, 2016: 49–52), and linked to an international brand that conferred the imprimatur of comfort on the site (Morrison, 2016: 57–58). During the vicissitudes of the late 1980s, the collapse of the Berlin Wall and the rise of irredentist nationalism in the former Yugoslavia, the hotel's role changed. It became a political space associated initially with the Serbian nationalist Social Democratic Party (SDS), and was later shared by the international bodies implicated in the internationalisation of conflict resolution: the United Nations Protection Force and the European Community Monitor Mission teams. Morrison (2016) offers a detailed rendering of the hotel as a space of intrigue and interaction. His analysis is less explicitly focused on explicating the mediating potentials of hotel spatial regimes, but he offers a valuable survey of hotels as sites of conflict in the early chapters of his book, as well as an analysis of the func-tions ascribed to hotels by Fregonese and Ramadan (2015). He charts its experience sequentially from SDS-dominated political space to a press hotel so ably discussed by Smirl (2016). In this respect, the Holiday Inn Sarajevo emerges as one of the most thoroughly studied hotels in a conflict zone.

Cairene Hotels in an Era of Civil Strife

Tracing the experience of Cairo's Shepheard's Hotel in the previous chapter, and earlier in this chapter, we have seen how an establishment founded in the 1850s was legitimated as a target of Egyptian nationalism in 1952. The framing of the hotel as a bastion of external power illustrated the entwinement of hotel development and anti-colonialism. As Maurizio Peleggi (2012: 125–126) has noted, the incubation of hostility towards European hegemons intensified in many places in the interwar period, even as the colonial grand hotel appeared to telegraph stability and supply spaces of familiarity to the European settler and travelling populations. The experiences of hotels during the Egyptian revolution underlined ways in which they were implicated in assaults on a political regime that was associated with systems of coercive, external, Western political and eco-nomic power. An examination of Shepheard's Hotel over the course of many decades has the advantage of illustrating how changes in the geopo-litical environment resulted in its enrolment within a variety of pro-grammes – its construction as a project connected to British-financed tourism development in the colonial period, its complex role as a mediat-ing institution and site of local elite sociability in the era of British suzerainty, and its obliteration as a signifier of the end of the colonial era in 1952. Participants in the 1952 revolution targeted a number of buildings in the capital that were seen as symbols of British colonialism: Shepheard's Hotel's destruction was a monumental signifier of the assault on colonialism. Yesser Elsheshtawy (2014: 413) interprets the hotel as signifying the social, cultural and economic relations of domination that critics associated with the British state. The hotel's famous guests had included prominent Western writers and politicians, including Teddy Roosevelt. It was part of an urban fabric that had been considerably transformed since the great fire of 1846, including the development of European-inscribed landscape in the form of extensive, Parisian-style boulevards. Its terrace and bar were among the most famous points of congregation for urban elites. Moreover, its design articulated a degree of social and cultural distance: Elsheshtawy (2014) argues that the hotel, with its elevated terrace and distinctive spatial regimes, promoted social relations that expressed its distance and disconnectedness from Cairine life – an aspect of hotel culture and design that it shared with other 'Western'-style institutions of commercial accommodation in the city, and which made it susceptible to de-territorialisation and later to identification as a citadel of colonialism. The conflagration that laid the groundwork for the development of 'modern' Cairo in 1846 was exceeded, if not in its architectural impact, then in its political symbolism, in January 1952, when the city centre was engulfed in flames as a fire was ignited during protests at the iconic Casino Opera. It spread to, and claimed, other landmarks, including cinemas and hotels. Colonial-era hotels and other buildings were symbols of a system of political power to which the revolutionary ideology was responding and which it was repudiating. Elsheshtawy argues that this phase of the revolution is critical for understanding the ways in which the built environment was implicated in the critique of a programme of 'modernisation' that had roots in the 19th-century alliance between the Egyptian state and Western, especially British, powers. This reading of the urban hotel's colonialist symbolisms is extended into the analysis of the urban hotel topography's reconfiguration in a new political environment, guided by the economic and political priorities of the Nasserite state, when hotels were assigned new roles and assumed new forms within the context of Cold War geopolitics.

The post-revolutionary building programme in Cairo has been regarded as an expression of Nasser's pan-Arabist, socialist ideology – one that was deliberately distanced from symbols and markers of the colonial relationship with Britain and instead centred on projects that proclaimed openness to new partnerships in the Arab world and beyond (Elsheshtawy,

2013). Hotel building was also part of an effort to develop the tourism sector and attract trade and foreign currency from the West, and the post-revolutionary state's commitment to hotel building included, perhaps ironically, the construction of a new Shepheard's Hotel (Azmy & Atef, 2011). The erection of the Cairo Hilton (Figure 5.4) was also part of this programmatic effort to promote tourism, and also project stability and prestige (Azmy & Atef, 2011: 227–237). It involved close collaboration between Hilton International, the Egyptian state and state-sanctioned parties that financed the hotel's construction, with Hilton deeply involved in efforts to facilitate completion of the establishment. The hotel's construction began soon after the revolution. Its completion was complicated by the Suez Crisis in 1956. The US, while disapproving of its French and British allies' military intervention, imposed economic sanctions and adopted other punitive measures against Egyptian interests. It finally opened in 1959.

While Noha Osman Azmy and Tamer Mohamed Atef (2011) explain the hotel's fitful start largely in relation to the imperatives and priorities of the post-revolutionary state, and the disrupting influences of the Suez conflict, Annabel Wharton (2001) analyses the architecture of the Nile

Figure 5.4 Nile Hilton construction, 1950s

Hilton in terms of how it articulated an American-driven modernism and hegemony. In this respect, the hotel is studied as a legible marker of a new political order – as much as the smouldering ruins of Shepheard's Hotel were in 1952. Its physical positioning, and its American-designed architectural style, both telegraphed and moulded ideas about America and Egypt – and, implicitly, the historical European colonial project. Elsheshtawy (2013: 355) notes that from its inception in the first year after the revolution, the Hilton was imagined as a counterpoint to the historical aesthetics and symbolisms of Shepheard's Hotel. In his reading of the building, which is at odds with Wharton's claim that its orientation had the effect of effacing the Islamic city by 'backing onto it', Elsheshtawy contends that the old city was too distant to be visible. He also challenges Wharton's claim that the interior lobby's spatial organisation reinforced the negation of the old city, instead arguing that its form was largely functional (Elsheshtawy, 2013: 357). The two studies of the hotel's interior share a reading of the symbolic functions of the Pharonic décor, which compressed the temporal and spatial distance between Ancient Egypt and the modern West (Elsheshtawy, 2013: 357), and projected a distinctive message about the character of Egyptian modernity. The functional features of the hotel extended this ideological position – especially through social practices which promoted conspicuous display within the hostelry (Elsheshtawy, 2013: 358), and offered a venue for the Egyptian elite, as well as for travellers, journalists and others, as it became deeply embedded within the social and cultural life of the city. During the 1967 war with Israel, it offered a site of refuge, and its status was reconfigured from a place of elite Egyptian culture to one of shelter for non-Egyptians. These roles changed the hotel's place in the public imagination before it resumed its central place in the regional geopolitics, hosting the Jordanian and PLO leaders after the 1970 Black September massacre, as Nasser aimed to play a mediating role (Elsheshtawy, 2013: 361).

Shepheard's Hotel and the Nile Hilton are prominent cases of sites that were conceived and built in markedly different geopolitical environments – on either side of the watershed of 1952. The lifespan of a third establishment, the Continental Hotel, spanned the revolution. It was thus embedded neither within the narratives of the comprehensive repudiation of British colonialism through physical destruction and reconstruction after 1952, nor the erection of a new establishment, the Hilton, whose aesthetics, location and form were grounded in the geopolitical contexts of the Cold War era. Like Shepheard's Hotel, the Continental Hotel was a target of the January 1952 riots, but it was reopened the following year under the operation of the Anglo-American Nile Co. and the ownership of the Société des Grand Hotels d'Egypte, both of which were engaged in the hotel business elsewhere in Egypt (Azmy & Atef, 2011: 237). The reopening of the hotel was part of a deliberate effort to create a new tourist infrastructure in post-1952 Egypt. Its hotels would attract and reassure travellers after the traumatic and dramatic events of the revolution. The state intervened actively to promote these goals. Its 'modernisation' was realised through new systems of classification, staff training and financing agreements, such as that arranged between Bank Misr and Hilton International, in which the state pursued a multi-pronged strategy of post-revolutionary normalisation, improvement and promotion through hotel development. Although many historical case studies reveal the physical transformation and symbolic transfiguration of institutions associated with the colonial period, another institution – the Nile Hilton – was a product of a postwar geopolitical environment dominated by a bipolar world.

Hotels in the Cold War

As the Cairene hotel histories suggest, the commercial and political priorities of American interests, and American cultural influences, shaped the hotel topographies of many former European colonial spaces in outsize ways. This leads us to explore the role of the hotel not in places of violent conflagration, but instead in sites of continuous contest between two dominant world actors, the US and the USSR, in which they vied to win the support of regimes, and to construct and project their values after World War II. Technologies and innovations in service and spatial organisation, long associated with American exceptionalism, were critical to these developments. Annabel Wharton (2001) has shown that hotels were enrolled in the projection of American soft power during the Cold War, in which the signature plate-glass design element of the international Hilton constituted an aesthetic of American modernism and efficiency in urban landscapes. Hilton hotels were erected in a variety of ways that were influenced by local contexts, sometimes with exoticised 'native' inflected interior design, such as those of its Istanbul and Cairo locations. The physical orientation of buildings was symbolically crucial – towards the markers of 'Ancient' Cairo, the Acropolis in Athens and the Americanised western quarter of Berlin (Wharton, 2011: 27, 66). Wharton's dissection of the structure and meaning of the Istanbul Hilton, opened in 1955, for example, identifies how the monumental, reinforced concrete building, located on an elevated preserve above Galata, signalled the continuous evolution of the city, and the strong association between modernism, the Hilton hotel and the articulation of American values and influence. However, Wharton (2001: 26–27) notes, as elsewhere where 'local' elements figured into design, that Turkish motifs were critical to interior décor.

These architectural and design features were part of a programmatic effort to project interwoven corporate and strategic national priorities in the postcolonial environment. The US government and Conrad Hilton exploited hotels' privileged positions in urban locations to propound ideas about America, its relationship to the local culture, and the primacy of its values in the context of what it portrayed as a global struggle against tyranny. Cities were sites in which this programme was articulated. The Habana Hilton (Figure 5.5) also assumed strategic value during the early years of the Cold War. However, in charting the nuanced private diplomacy in which Hilton was a major actor, Dennis Merrill (2009) has shown that the establishment's final 'fall' to Fidel Castro's revolutionaries during the consolidation of the Cuban Revolution was not a moment of sudden takeover that coincided with the city's own capture, as many narratives of hotel 'conquests' contend, but rather the endgame in a series of lengthy diplomatic and political engagements through which the hotel remained open to travellers, financed in fact by the revolutionary state, during which Hilton International and the American administration pursued decidedly different strategies. Hilton's pragmatism in engaging Castro and his government in meetings (many hosted in the hotel itself) were efforts to avoid a political confrontation, to gauge the extent of Castro's interest in developing a true command economy model, and to explore how Hilton's corporate identity and interests might be advanced in the context of the revolution. Only when the weight of the revolutionaries' deep-seated resentment of the regional hegemon, which for decades had been expressed through a tourist relationship in which Cuba was portrayed as a warm playground for the American holidaymaker, did stresses induced by the revolution prove irresolvable. The $24 million, 558-room hotel, then the largest in Latin America, became such a flashpoint in Cuban-US relations that its belated nationalisation marked a landmark moment in the collapse of the precarious relationship between the two states, its subordination starkly signalling the triumph of the Cuban revolutionary programme over American dominance.

Conclusion

Beirut and Sarajevo supply historians with examples of 20th-century conflicts in which hotels participated in civil breakdown, while Egypt,

Figure 5.5 Advertisement for the opening of the Habana Hilton, 1958

Cuba and other places furnish examples of how they became key actors in global geopolitics. They underline the value of examining hotels as participants actively shaping the contours of conflicts in other, especially earlier, places and time periods. In Ireland, for example, during both the 1916 uprising against the British state, and also during the 1922–23 civil war over the terms of the treaty that partitioned the island, hotels were prominent casualties of urban warfare. Many of Dublin's most famous hostelries were commandeered or laid to waste. While the targeting of Belfast's Europa Hotel and Brighton's Grand Hotel during the years of the Troubles is well known (Morrison, 2016: 15–26), the experience of hotels during these earlier conflicts reveal how the places of commercial accommodation became embroiled in the prosecution of urban combat. They were not symbolic, prestige targets as much as tactical assets: indeed, they served as command and control infrastructures integral to the prosecution of the conflicts. Their roles in these conflicts, for which there is an especially vivid visual record (Figures 5.6, 5.7, 5.8, 5.9) remain to be clarified, but their selective targeting and destruction were central to contemporary representations of a ravaged city, and to the collapse of many of its core institutions.

In addition to expanding the empirical base by incorporating more historical case studies for testing Fregonese and Ramadan's claims about hotels and conflict, it is helpful to widen the temporal and geographic compass to embrace hotels in wartime that are not located in zones of conflict. War implicated hotels in places where bullets fly and lines are

Figure 5.6 Wynn's Hotel, Abbey Street, Dublin, 1916

Figure 5.7 Metropole Hotel shelled, Dublin, 1916

Figure 5.8 Granville Hotel ruins, O'Connell Street, Dublin, 1922

Figure 5.9 Gresham Hotel, Dublin ablaze: War in Ireland. 2 July 1922

drawn through cities to demarcate the territories of belligerents. But in places that were not theatres of war, the hotel could serve as a nerve-centre for ordering and prosecuting conflict from a distance. They were susceptible to being commandeered and adapted for such purposes because of their size and central location. In London, and in other cities, many large hotels were requisitioned during conflicts such as World War I, to accommodate the apparatus of the state. Miami and Miami Beach hotels were repurposed during World War II for military training and other roles (Denfeld, 2007). Hotels in non-belligerent states were also critical to the shaping of wars, not least through their functions as sites of refuge within neutral political environments. Hansruedi Müller and Anna Amacher Hoppler (2013), for example, have explored hotels in Switzerland, which was not a belligerent in either world war. Its commercial hospitality sector was nonetheless profoundly shaped by the conflicts. During the late 19th century, tourism became a critical element of the Swiss economy, disproportionately focused on the luxury hotel market. Though neutral, Switzerland's sector was profoundly – and in some cases irreversibly – changed with the onset of hostilities, with the grand hotel segment, and its pricing policies, severely impacted during World War I. Müller and Hoppler (2013: 116) argue that grand hotels were dealt a blow during this period from which they never fully recovered. As Germany prepared for conflict in the 1930s, Switzerland entered into an agreement whereby the purchase of German coal exports would enable tourists to continue to visit the country (Müller & Hoppler, 2013: 112). During the second global conflict, hotels in the neutral country were used for a variety of purposes: by army personnel, and as camps for refugees – a function that grew in importance as the war continued (Müller & Hoppler, 2013: 114–115), when the sector's strategic financial value was realised in terms of the favourable balance of trade to which it could contribute. Fulfilling one of Fregonenese and Ramadan's (2015) roles assigned to hotels, Switzerland also supplied places for postwar political negotiations, their suitability for such purposes shaped by the neutral status of the country (Müller & Hoppler, 2013: 116). Müller and Hoppler contend that although Swiss hotels were not impacted by war in the same way as establishments that were at the centre of conflict zones, or located in the capital of hostile countries, their functions were nonetheless profoundly influenced by the outbreak and unfolding of hostilities. Their histories suggest a more expansive analysis of how conditions of war produce dramatically new circumstances for hotels in non-belligerent states – beginning with, but not limited to, the influx of civilians seeking refuge from theatres of conflict, where the hotel offers refuge, but leaving it is often impossible.

An expansion of the scope and scale of research on wartime hotels could include the analysis of the historical development of establishments within urban topographies, associated with specific political regimes, to explore how symbolisms accrue to them. Sara Fregonese (2012) has under-scored the relationship between spatial patterns in the city which promote the hotel's de-territorialisation. Combined with the global networks within which the hotel participates, those historical processes can become germane to its experience of, and enrolment in, urban violence. A more systematic study of wartime leisure, and the role of the hotel within it, would also be instructive. Hotels had critical functions supplying sites of respite and leisure: hotels that were not in the crosshairs, or at the centre of conflict zones, for example, offered places of resort to military person-nel on leave (Lisle, 2016). Through an analysis of these places, we can develop a broader understanding of the hotel's capacities to operate in adaptive ways, rather than merely studying them in terms of the disrup-tions that war brings to their conventional roles. It also allows us to knit together the three key themes explored in this book and develop a more precise understanding of how an establishment's history – whether as a creation of colonial capital, or as part of a Western brand – becomes criti-cal to the symbolisms hostile actors inscribe in it during wartime.

6 Conclusion

This goal of this book has been to introduce readers to selected concerns in hotel scholarship, focusing on: (1) the American hotel as a social technology, a site of technological innovation and an institution at the vanguard of American dominance of the global commercial hospitality sector after World War II; (2) the hotel's protean and nuanced identities in colonial and postcolonial environments; and (3) the hotel as an actor in urban conflict zones, enrolled materially and symbolically in diverse ways. These research agendas treat urban contexts as integral to producing the modern hotel, and tend in each case towards treating diverse establishments as part of a single institution. The modern hotel, as we have seen in all three cases, is also largely studied as part of the networks of modern, urban life, facilitating flows of capital, people and information. There are a number of heuristic points explored but not remedied in this book that would repay close attention. The scope of this study, for one, invites extension: during the period under examination here, there were innovations in lodging forms and functions in Europe, including the *paradore* in Spain (Diez-Pastor, 2010; Pack, 2006), the *pusada* network developed in Portugal in the 1940s, which often repurposed historic buildings, and the adapted 'country house hotel' in the UK and Ireland. All three demand attention, and would be fruitfully integrated into a critical history of the European hostelry in the 20th century. The incorporation of the vibrant historiography and theoretical literature on German hotels, and also Swiss and French institutions, would be invaluable. Beyond this expanded scope of analysis, there are tantalising ways in which a more holistic approach to hotel history might upend the shibboleths reviewed here. One consequence of associating the hotel with Western space, for example, is the reification of non-Western places. A trope in the narrative of the rise of the grand hotel, for example, is an allusion to, and Orientalist framings of, Silk Road caravanserais, framed as the hotel's ancient, but decidedly obsolete, precursors. An approach which de-centres the Western hotel in the narrative of commercial accommodation's modernisation and also pays close attention to the ways in which the caravanserai as an institution was handled in 19th-century discourse on the Western hotel would redress this persistent problem of framing the institution's evolution.

There are other lacunae in the study of modern hotels that many scholars are actively addressing. Interest in rural, non-Western colonial environments has largely focused on accommodation and leisure infrastructures that responded to discourses of the health-giving properties of water and air in the colonies, leading Europeans to resort to them *because of* the natural environment, and thereby reproduce practices that had long histories in Europe. Eric T. Jennings (2007) and others (Kenny, 1995) have ably explored places in which resorts offered refuges *from* the colonial environments – and particularly from climates deemed to be potentially injurious to the health of the colonist. Studying the French colonial hill station, for example, Jennings underlines that it is easy to become entranced by the story of the urban grand hotel and its ostentatious symbolism, and by a narrative that treats it as an inscription of metropolitan modernity and culture in the colonial milieu. But he reminds us that there were a host of other sites, including many that catered to mixed populations and to settlers, outside this metropolitan regime, where identity and status were negotiated in their everyday operations (Jennings, 2003, 2007). The agenda that Jennings has set for the French colonial hill stations could be pursued by scholars elsewhere, inviting systematic comparative analysis across colonial worlds.

The dominant focus of hotel history on institutions of a large – and growing – scale, epitomised by the grand hotel, also has implications for the framing of other forms of Western commercial accommodation, and for critically engaging with discourses that configured them as foils to the modern hotel. As we have seen earlier in this study, as commentators breathlessly charted the American hotel's rise, an antiquarian discourse developed a rhetorical counterpoint: nostalgia-infused rhapsodies for the rustic, familiar, timeless, country hostelry. Part of the relentless logic of the hotel system was allegedly a subordination of guests to a regime in which their identity was reduced to that of a room number (Hayner, 1928: 789; Hayner, 1936). This depersonalisation was regarded as an inevitable consequence of the advanced commercialisation – even industrialisation – of modern hospitality. Writers located an enduring alternative to this trajectory under the timber beams of the English country inn. While this framing of the institutions was pervasive in the last decades of the 19th and first decades of the 20th centuries, critical engagement with it has been remarkably limited. Charlotte Bates (2003) has noted that the panegyric to the English country inn was especially resonant in the interwar period (2003: 67), when the diffusion of the automobile enabled more and more people to penetrate the English countryside, when an acute sense of rootlessness and nomadism infiltrated popular imagination, and when sentimental narratives of Old England were manifested in the accounts of such travel writers as H.V. Morton (Perry, 1999). Yet they were accompanied by a sometimes-deliberate effort to tap nostalgia through the erection of new commercial accommodation in the pseudo-old inn style. These observations raise two points worthy of great attention: why was the 'English' inn configured in such a way – more so, it seems, than in its Scottish counterpart, for example? And how did such discourses intersect with the marketing of travel and lodging, the inn becoming integrated within, rather than standing apart from, the evolving structures of commercial accommodation. Even in America, where the modern hotel was said to epitomise the sector's relentless technologisation and rationalisation, the automobile offered a fillip to taverns and inns, which were burnished for the new arrivals, just as tea-rooms, sometimes in repurposed barns, restaurants, new roadside motor courts, and even gas stations, embraced both the travellers and often a traditional colonial aesthetic (Rhoads, 1986). Scholarship on the deep emotional investment in 'traditional' lodging forms in other places (Gyimóthy, 2005) could guide this research agenda away from an Anglo-American focus.

There is also a tendency in focusing on the large American hotel as a representative lodging to occlude other forms, including rural hotels, and to obscure enduring influences that earlier forms of accommodation had over it, especially in the colonial period. Daniel Maudlin (James *et al.*, 2016) has charted the evolution of the American inn and hotels and underscores elements of functional and aesthetic continuity between the early-modern and modern periods. His findings challenge the idea that the hotel emerged as a distinctive institution in the late 18th century. Indeed, Maudlin draws out critical contrasts between the historical, discursive constructions of the inn and tavern and evidence of their dynamic and evolving character. Maudlin offers a timely and important re-evaluation of the periodisation of the hotel's 'birth' and of its institutional uniqueness that will shed light on similar co-constructions elsewhere, since the production of a binary through the lens of the hotel's modernity is not limited to the English-speaking world.

In the heyday of the hotel, commentators rhapsodised about this peculiar 'city within a city' and likened it to a finely-tuned machine. That vision of the hotel bears directly on the study of the colonial hotel, whose functions, forms and symbolisms have evolved in postcolonial environments, reinforcing their mutability and their status as sites of contest. In the postcolonial period, the hotel has been enlisted in a variety of projects, from anti-colonialist politics to heritage programmes. Studying ways in which the colonial hotel in particular has become embroiled in violent conflicts, with its historical institutional evolution bearing directly on the associations and meanings that have been ascribed to it, would reveal competing inscriptions in the hotel, including those that authorise its physical obliteration, and others its preservation, and would deepen our understanding of how its material form and its contested symbolisms have been shaped by historical networks and flows of capital, information and people.

Drawing these strands of analysis together, the hotel emerges as a locus of place-, identity- and history-making, central to the historical processes of urbanisation, technologisation, industrial capitalism, colonialism, nationalism and globalisation. As recent decades have not only witnessed the intensified mobilisation of hotel history in the production of hotel heritage, hotels have also moved towards an embrace of kitsch and flamboyant simulacra which revel in the mutability of the hotel's identity, form and symbolisms, underscoring this through the playful 'replication' of hotels in new environments – at Disney properties, for instance, hotels have become central to the experience of fantasyscapes. Nowhere is this more apparent than in Las Vegas, where Jeffrey Cass (2004) locates 'postmodern Orientalism' and George Ritzer and Todd Stillman (2001) see the apotheosis of the spectacularisation of hotels, in which conventional, historical boundaries and spatial and temporal orders associated with them, are playfully inverted. Amid the kitsch and simulacra, hotels' obsolescence is foreordained, as they inhabit a city that embraces creative reinvention. A survey of the hotel's treatment as a singular institution that has been consistently treated as manifesting Western modernity ends with open questions: does this emergence of the 'postmodern hotel' suggest that the lifespan of the 'modern' hotel, as it has been understood and studied in the scholarship surveyed here, may have finally has reached an end? What new possibilities emerge for hotels' meanings and representations?

References

Sources Published Before 1945

The Caterer, Hotel Keeper and Refreshment Contractor's Gazette (London).

Caterer, Hotel Keeper and Restaurateurs' Gazette (London).

Chambers's Encyclopaedia: A Dictionary of Universal Knowledge for the People (1875). vol. 5, American ed., rev. Philadelphia: J.B. Lippincott & Co.

Cornyn, W.S. (1939) Hotel slang. *American Speech* 14 (3), 239–240.

Hayner, N.S. (1928) Hotel life and personality. *American Journal of Sociology* 33 (5), 784–795.

Hayner, N.S. (1936) *Hotel Life.* Chapel Hill: University of North Carolina Press.

Hotels. (1856) *North British Review.* American ed. 24 (48), 269–286.

Hotel Monthly (Chicago)

James, H. (1907) *The American Scene.* London: Chapman & Hall.

Keesey, W.M. (1927) *Tales of Old Inns. The History, Legend and Romance of Some of our Older* Hostelries. London: Trust Houses.

Kracauer, S. (2004) The Hotel Lobby. From *The Mass Ornament: Weimar Essays, 1922–25.* In M. Miles and I. Borden (eds) *The Cities Culture Reader* (2nd edn). London: Routledge.

Maskell, H.P. and Edward, W.G. (1910) *Old Country Inns of England.* London: I. Pitman.

Modern hotels (August 1873) *Scribner's Monthly* 6 (4), 486–492.

Modern hotels (24 September 1898) *Chambers's Journal*, 6th series 1 (43), 673–675.

Reynolds-Ball, E.A.B. (1897) *Cairo: City of the Caliphs. A Popular Study of Cairo and its Environs and the Nile and its Antiquities.* Boston: Dana Estes and Company.

Sala, G.A. (1861) American hotels and American food. *Temple Bar Magazine* 2, 345–356.

Trollope, A. (1862) *North America.* New York: Harper and Brothers, Publishers.

Williamson, J. (1930) *The American Hotel: An Anecdotal History.* New York: A.A. Knopf.

Willcock, J.W. (1829) *The Laws Relating to Inns, Hotels, Alehouses, and Places of Public Entertainment: To Which is Added, An Abstract of the Statute for the Regulation of Post Horses.* London: Hodson, printer; Saunders and Benning, Law Booksellers.

Morning Post (London)

London Illustrated News

Sources Published After 1945

Aburish, S.K. (1989) *The St George Hotel Bar.* London: Bloomsbury.

Anderson, M. (2012) The development of British tourism in Egypt, 1815 to 1850. *Journal of Tourism History* 4 (3), 259–279.

Armstead, M.B.Y. (1999) 'Lord, Please Don't Take Me in August': African–Americans in Newport and Saratoga Springs, 1870–1930. Urbana and Chicago: University of Illinois Press.

Armstead, M.B.Y. (2005) Revisiting hotels and other lodgings: American tourist spaces through the lens of black travellers. Journal of Decorative and Propaganda Arts 25, 136–159.

Arslan, A. and Polat, H.A. (2015) The Ottoman Empire's first attempt to establish hotels in İstanbul: The Ottoman Imperial Hotels Company. Tourism Management (51), 103–111.

Auer, J. (2013) Queerest little city in the world: Gay Reno in the sixties. Journal of Homosexuality 60 (1), 16–30.

Avermaete, T. (2013) The architectonics of the hotel lobby: The norms and forms of a public-private figure. In T. Avermaete and A. Massey (eds) Hotel Lobbies and Lounges (pp. 59–71). Abingdon: Routledge.

Avermaete, T. and Massey, A. (2013) Hotel Lobbies and Lounges: The Architecture of Professional Hospitality. Abingdon: Routledge.

Azmy, N.O. and Atef, T.M. (2011) The Egyptian government's role in re-establishing the hotel industry in Cairo (1953–1957). International Journal of Hospitality & Tourism Administration 12 (3), 225–251.

Bates, C. (2003) Hotel histories: Modern tourists, modern nomads and the culture of hotel-consciousness. Literature & History 12 (2), 62–75.

Battilani, P. and Fauri, F. (2009) The rise of a service-based economy and its transformation: Seaside tourism and the case of Rimini. Journal of Tourism History 1 (1), 27–48.

Baum, J.A.C. and Ingram, P. (1998) Survival-enhancing learning in the Manhattan hotel industry, 1898–1980. Management Science 44 (7), 996–1016.

Baum, J.A.C. and Mezias, S.J. (1992) Localized competition and organizational failure in the Manhattan hotel industry, 1898–1990. Administrative Science Quarterly 37 (4), 580–604.

Bayley, S. (2010) Home on the Horizon: America's Search for Space, from Emily Dickinson to Bob Dylan. Witney, Oxfordshire: Peter Lang.

Belasco, W.J. (1979) Americans on the Road: From Motorcamp to Motel, 1910–1945. Cambridge, MA: MIT Press.

Bennett, B.T. (2007) Understanding, Assessing, and Responding to Terrorism: Protecting Critical Infrastructure and Personnel. Hoboken, NJ: A. John Wiley & Sons, Inc.

Berens, C. (1997) Hotel Bars and Lobbies. New York: McGraw-Hill.

Berger, M.W. (2005a) The American hotel. Journal of Decorative and Propaganda Arts 25, 6–9.

Berger, M.W. (2005b) The rich man's city: Hotels and mansions of Gilded Age New York. Journal of Decorative and Propaganda Arts 25, 46–71.

Berger, M.W. (2011) Hotel Dreams: Luxury, Technology, and Urban Ambition in America, 1829–1929. Baltimore: The Johns Hopkins University Press.

Boana, C. and Chabarek, D. (2013) A stroll down memory lane - the Battle of the Hotels. The Journal of Space Syntax 4 (1), 130–135.

Boorstin, D.J. (1965) The Americans: The National Experience. New York: Random House.

Boorstin, D.J. (1973) The Americans: The Democratic Experience. New York; Random House.

Borsay, P. and Walton, J.K. (eds) (2011) *Resorts and Ports: European Seaside Towns since 1700*. Bristol: Channel View Publications.

Braden, S.R. (2002) *The Architecture of Leisure: The Florida Resort Hotels of Henry Flagler and Henry Plant*. Gainesville: University of Florida Press.

Branchik, B.J. (2002) Out in the market: A history of the gay market segment in the United States. *Journal of Macromarketing* 22 (1), 86–97.

Bremner, H. (2013) Tourism development in the Hot Lakes District, New Zealand c. 1900. *International Journal of Contemporary Hospitality Management* 25 (2), 282–298.

Brody, D. (2010) *Visualizing American Empire: Orientalism and Imperialism in the Philippines*. Chicago and London: University of Chicago Press.

Brucken, C. (1996) In the public eye: Women and the American luxury hotel. *Winterthur Portfolio* 31 (4), 203–220.

Bruegmann, R. (1997) *The Architects and the City: Holabird & Roche of Chicago, 1880–1918*. Chicago: University of Chicago Press.

Calvert, D. and Lambert, R.A. (1997) A Highland hotel venture: The case of the Doune of Rothiemurchus, 1935–1942. *Northern Scotland* 17 (1), 153–172.

Carmouche, R. (1980) Social Class in Hotels. Paper presented at the Autumn Symposium of the International Association of Hotel Management Schools, Huddersfield, UK.

Cass, J. (2004) Egypt on steroids: Luxor Las Vegas and postmodern Orientalism. In D.M. Lasansky and B. McLaren (eds) *Architecture and Tourism: Perception, Performance and Place* (pp. 241–263). Oxford and New York: Berg.

Chambers, T.A. (2001) *Drinking the Waters: Creating an American Leisure Class at Nineteenth-Century Mineral Springs*. Washington: Smithsonian Institution Press.

Chang, T.C. and Teo, P. (2009) The shophouse hotel: Vernacular heritage in a creative city. *Urban Studies* 26 (2), 341–367.

Chang, J., Ryan, C., Tsai, Chen-Tsang, S. and Wen, Hsuan-Ying, S. (2012) The Taiwanese love motel–an escape from leisure constraints? *International Journal of Hospitality Management* 31 (1), 169–179.

Chaplin, S. (2007) *Japanese Love Hotels: A Cultural History*. Abingdon: Routledge.

Chisholm, B., Floren, R. and Gutsche, A. (2001) *Castles of the North: Canada's Grand Hotels*. Toronto: Lynx Images Inc.

Clarke, J. (2002) Like a huge birdcage exhaled from the earth: Watson's Esplanade Hotel, Mumbai (1867–71), and its place in structural history. *Construction History* 18, 37–77.

Clarke, D.B., Pfannhauser, V.C. and Doel, M.A. (eds) (2009) *Moving Pictures/Stopping Places: Hotels and Motels on Film*. Lanham: Lexington Books.

Cocks, C. (2001) *Doing the Town: The Rise of Urban Tourism in the United States, 1850–1915*. Berkeley: University of California Press.

Conlin, M.V. and Bird, G.R. (2014) *Railway Heritage and Tourism*. Bristol: Channel View Publications.

Cook, M. (2003) *London and the Culture of Homosexuality, 1885–1914*. Cambridge: Cambridge University Press.

Cossic, A. and Galliou, P. (eds) (2006) *Spas in Britain and in France in the Eighteenth and Nineteenth Centuries*. Newcastle: Cambridge Scholars Publishing.

Craggs, R. (2012) Towards a political geography of hotels: Southern Rhodesia, 1958–1962. *Political Geography* 31 (4), 215–224.

Crook, T. (2008) Accommodating the outcast: Common lodging houses and the limits of urban governance in Victorian and Edwardian London. *Urban History* 35 (3), 414–436.

Czyzewska, B. and Roper, A. (2017) A foreign hotel in London–the history of Hilton's negotiation of legitimacy in the Swinging Sixties. *Hospitality & Society* 7 (3), 219–244.

Davidson, L.P. (2005a) 'A service machine': Hotel guests and the development of an early-twentieth-century building type. In K.A. Breisch and A.K. Hoagland (eds) *Building Environments: Perspectives in Vernacular Architecture*, (Vol. 10, pp. 113–132). Knoxville: University of Tennessee Press.

Davidson, L.P. (2005b) Twentieth-century hotel architects and the origins of standardization. *Journal of Decorative and Propaganda Arts* 25, 72–103.

Davidson, R.A. (2006) A periphery with a view: Hotel space and the Catalan modern experience. *Romance Quarterly* 53 (3), 169–183.

Davidson, R.A. (2018) *The Hotel: Occupied Space*. Toronto: University of Toronto Press.

de Grèce, M., Meade, Martin, F.J. and Lawrence, A. (1987) *Grand Oriental Hotels*. London: Dent.

Denby, E. (1998) *Grand Hotels: Reality and Illusion: An Architectural and Social History*. London: Reaktion Books.

Denfeld, D.C. (2007) Isely Field: World War II in the Pacific. *Journal of America's Military Past* 33 (2), 72–90.

DePastino, T. (2003) *Citizen Hobo: How a Century of Homelessness Shaped America*. Chicago: University of Chicago Press.

Dhingra, P. (2012) *Life Behind the Lobby: Indian American Motel Owners and the American Dream*. Stanford: Stanford University Press.

Diez-Pastor, M.C. (2010) 'Albergues de carretera' (highway inns): A key step in the evolution of Spanish tourism and modernist architecture. *Journal of Tourism History* 2 (1), 1–22.

Dolkart, A.S. (2005) Millionaires' elysiums: The luxury apartment hotels of Schultze and Weaver. *Journal of Decorative and Propaganda Arts* 25, 10–45.

Donzel, C., Gregory, A.G. and Walter, M. (1989) *Grand Hotels of North America*. Toronto: McClelland and Stewart Inc.

d'Ormesson, J. (1984) Introduction. In D. Watkin, H. Montgomery-Massingbred, P.-J. Rémy and F.c Grendel (eds) *Grand Hotel: The Golden Age of Palace Hotels. An Architectural and Social History* (pp. 7–11). New York and Paris: The Vendome Press.

Dubinsky, K. (1999) *The Second Greatest Disappointment: Honeymooning and Tourism at Niagara Falls*. Toronto: Between the Lines.

du Cros, H. (2004) Postcolonial conflict inherent in the involvement of cultural tourism in creating new national myths in Hong Kong. In C.M. Hall and H. Tucker (eds) *Tourism and Postcolonialism: Contested Discourses, Identities and Representations* (pp. 153–166). London and New York: Routledge.

Durie, A.D. with Bradley, J. and Dupree, M. (2006) *Water is Best: The Hydros and Health Tourism in Scotland, 1840–1940*. Edinburgh: John Donald.

Ebert, M.K. and Schmid, S. (eds) (2018) *Anglo-American Travelers and the Hotel Experience in Nineteenth-Century Literature: Nation, Hospitality, Travel Writing*. New York and Abingdon: Routledge.

Edensor, T. and Kothari, U. (2004) Sweetening colonialism: A Mauritian themed resort. In D.M. Lasansky and B. McLaren (eds) *Architecture and Tourism: Perception, Performance and Place* (pp. 189–205). Oxford and New York: Berg.

Elsheshtawy, Y. (2013) City interrupted: Modernity and architecture in Nasser's post-1952 Cairo. *Planning Perspectives* 28 (3), 347–371.

Elsheshtawy, Y. (2014) Urban transformations: The Great Cairo Fire and the founding of a modern capital, 1952–1950. *Built Environment* 40 (3), 408–425.

Fick, A. (2017) *New York Hotel Experience: Cultural and Societal Impacts of an American Invention*. Bielefeld: Transcript Verlag.

Fiévé, N. (2003) Pouvoir politique, modernité architecturale et paysage urbain dans le Japon de l'ère Meiji: l'hôtel Impérial de Tôkyô. In T. Sanjuan (dir.), *Les grands hôtels en Asie: modernité, dynamiques urbaines et sociabilité* (pp. 13–53). Paris, Publications de la Sorbonne.

Fiévé, N., Ged, F., Gelézeau, V., Guichard-Anguis, S. and Sanjuan, T. (2003) Introduction. In Thierry Sanjuan (dir.) *Les grands hôtels en Asie. Modernité, dynamiques urbaines et sociabilité* (pp. 5–10). Paris: Publications de la Sorbonne.

Firebaugh, W.C. (1972) *The Inns of Greece and Rome, and a History of Hospitality from the Dawn of Time to the Middle Ages*. New York: Benjamin Bloom (Original work published 1928).

Flint, J. (1983) Scandal at the Bristol Hotel: Some thoughts on racial discrimination in Britain and West Africa and its relationship to the planning of decolonisation, 1939–47. *The Journal of Imperial and Commonwealth History* 12 (1), 74–93.

Foster, M.S. (1999) In the face of 'Jim Crow': Prosperous blacks and vacations, travel and outdoor leisure, 1890–1945. *The Journal of Negro History* 84 (2), 130–149.

Fregonese, S. (2012) Between a refuge and a battleground: Beirut's discrepant cosmopolitanisms. *Geographical Review* 102 (3), 316–336.

Fregonese, S. and Ramadan, A. (2015) Hotel geopolitics: A research agenda. *Geopolitics* 20 (4), 793–813.

Fregonese, S. (2009) The urbicide of Beirut? Geopolitics and the built environment in the Lebanese civil war (1975–1976). *Political Geography* 28 (5), 309–318.

French, M. (2005) Commercials, careers, and culture: Travelling salesmen in Britain, 1890s–1930s. *The Economic History Review* 58 (2), 352–377.

French, M. (2010) On the road: Travelling salesmen and experiences of mobility in Britain before 1939. *The Journal of Transport History* 31 (2), 133–150.

Friedman, A.T. (2005) Merchandising Miami Beach: Morris Lapidus and the architecture of abundance. *Journal of Decorative and Propaganda Arts* 25, 216–253.

Frischauer, W. (1965) *A Hotel is Like A Woman: The Grand Hotels of Europe*. London: Leslie Frewin.

Frong, J. (2006) The horns of the dilemma: Race mixing and the enforcement of Jim Crow in New York City. *Journal of Urban History* 33 (1), 3–25.

Gamber, W. (2007) *The Boardinghouse in Nineteenth-Century America*. Baltimore: The Johns Hopkins University Press.

Gassen, R.H. (2008) *The Birth of American Tourism: New York, the Hudson Valley, and American Culture, 1790–1830*. Amherst: University of Massachusetts Press.

Gibson, S., Shapia, Y. and Chapman III, R.L. (2013) *Tourists, Travellers and Hotels in Nineteenth-Century Jerusalem*. Leeds: Maney Publishing.

Goh, D.P.S. (2010) Capital and the transfiguring monumentality of Raffles Hotel. *Mobilities* 5 (2), 177–195.

Graham, S. (2004) Cities as strategic sites: Place annihilation and urban geopolitics. In S. Graham (ed.) *Cities, War, and Terrorism: Towards an Urban Geopolitics* (pp. 31–53). Oxford: Blackwell Publishing.

Graham, T. (2014) *Mr. Flagler's St. Augustine*. Gainesville: University Press of Florida.

Groth, P. (1994) *Living Downtown: The History of Residential Hotels in the United States*. Berkeley: University of California Press.

Gyimóthy, S. (2005) Nostalgiascapes: The renaissance of Danish countryside inns. In T. O'Dell and P. Billing (eds) *Experiencescapes: Tourism, Culture and Economy* (pp. 112–124). Copenhagen: Cophenhagen Business School.

Hagglund, B. (2010) *Tourists and Travellers: Women's Non-fictional Writing about Scotland, 1770–1830*. Bristol: Channel View Publications.

Hall, C.M. and Tucker, H. (eds) (2004) *Tourism and Postcolonialism: Contested Discourses, Identities and Representations*. London and New York: Routledge.

Harismendy, P. (2016) D'une histoire de l'hôtellerie à celle de l'hospitalité? In J.-Y. Andrieux and P. Harismendy (eds) *Pension complete! Tourisme et hôtellerie (XVIIIe-XXe siècle)* (pp. 9–29). Rennes: Presses Universitaires de Rennes, 2016.

Hayes, S. (2014) A doomed business: The material culture of Ann Jones and the Glenrowan Inn. *Australasian Historical Archaeology* 32, 37–46.

Hazbun, W. (2007) The East as an exhibit: Thomas Cook & Son and the origins of the international tourism industry in Egypt. In P. Scranton and J.F. Davidson (eds) *The Business of Tourism: Place, Faith, and History* (pp. 3–33). Philadelphia: University of Pennsylvania Press.

Hembry, P.H. (1990) *The English Spa, 1560-1815: A Social History*. London: The Athlone Press.

Hembry, P.H., Cowie, L.W. and Cowie, E.E. (1997) *British Spas from 1815 to the Present: A Social History*. Madison: Fairleigh Dickinson University Press.

Henderson, J.C. (2001) Conserving colonial heritage: Raffles Hotel in Singapore. *International Journal of Heritage Studies* 7 (1), 7–24.

Henderson, J.C. (2004) Tourism and British colonial heritage in Malaysia and Singapore. In C.M. Hall and H. Tucker (eds) *Tourism and Postcolonialism: Contested Discourses, Identities and Representations* (pp. 113–125). London and New York: Routledge.

Henderson, J.C., Shufen, C., Huifen, L. and Xiang, L.L. (2010) Tourism and terrorism: A hotel industry perspective. *Journal of Tourism, Hospitality & Culinary Arts* 2 (1), 33–46.

Heynickx, R. (2015) Time in the hotel: Gazing with lobby lizards. *Interiors* 6 (2), 138–156.

Hoffman, D. (2005) The Brooksfields Hotel (Freetown, Sierra Leone). *Public Culture* 17 (1), 55–74.

Hoffman, D. (2007) The City as Barracks: Freetown, Monrovia, and the organization of violence in postcolonial African cities. *Cultural Anthropology* 22 (3), 400–428.

Horváth, Z. and Adrienne N. (2012) Baron for a day: Guests' perception of historical past in castle hotels. *Journal of Tourism Challenges and Trends* 5 (2), 103–123.

Hudson, C. (2009) Raffles Hotel Singapore: Advertising, consumption and romance. In D. Heng and S.M.K. Aljunied (eds) *Reframing Singapore Memory – Identity –Trans-Regionalism* (pp. 247–267). Amsterdam: Amsterdam University Press.

Humair, C. (2011) The hotel industry and its importance in the technical and economic development of a region: The Lake Geneva case (1852–1914). *Journal of Tourism History* 3 (3), 237–265.

Humphreys, A. (2011) *Grand Hotels of Egypt in the Golden Age of Travel*. Cairo: The American University of Cairo Press.

Hunter, F.R. (2004) Tourism and empire: The Thomas Cook & Son enterprise on the Nile, 1868–1914. *Middle Eastern Studies* 40 (5), 28–54.

Hunter, F.R. (2007) Promoting empire: The Hachette tourist in French Morocco, 1919–36. *Middle Eastern Studies* 43 (4), 579–591.

Ingram, P. (1996) Organizational form as a solution to the problem of credible commitment: The evolution of naming strategies among US hotel chains, 1896–1980. *Strategic Management Journal* 17 (S1), 85–98.

Jackson, A.A. (1998) The development of steel framed buildings in Britain, 1880–1905. *Construction History* 14, 21–40.

Jackson, A. (2013) *Buildings of Empire*. Oxford: Oxford University Press.

Jakle, J.A. Sculle, K.A. and Rogers, J.S. (1996) *The Motel in America*. The Johns Hopkins University Press.

James, K. (2012) '[A] British social institution': The visitors' book and hotel culture in Victorian Britain and Ireland. *Journeys: The International Journal of Travel and Travel Writing* 13 (1), 42–69.

James, K.J., Sandoval-Strausz, A.K., Maudlin, D., Peleggi, M., Humair, C. and Berger, M. (2017) The hotel in history: Evolving perspectives. *Journal of Tourism History* 9 (1), 92–111.

Jameson, F. (1991) *Postmodernism, Or, The Cultural Logic of Late Capitalism*. Durham, NC: Duke University Press.

Jennings, E.T. (2003) From *Indochine* to *Indochic*: The Lang Bian/Dalat Palace Hotel and French colonial leisure, power and culture. *Modern Asian Studies* 37 (1), 159–194.

Jennings, E.T. (2007) *Curing the Colonizers: Hydrotherapy, Climatology, and French Colonial Spas*. Durham, NC: Duke University Press.

Jim, Bernard, L. (2005) 'Wrecking the joint': The razing of city hotels in the first half of the twentieth century. *Journal of Decorative and Propaganda Arts* 25, 288–315.

Katz, M. (1999) The hotel Kracauer. *differences [sic]: A Journal of Feminist Cultural Studies* 11 (2), 134–152.

Kalman, H.D. (1968) *The Railway Hotels and the Development of the Château Style in Canada*. Victoria: University of Victoria Maltwood Museum.

Kenny, J.T. (1995) Climate, race, and imperial authority: The symbolic landscape of the British hill station in India. *Annals of the Association of American Geographers* 85 (4), 694–714.

King, A.D. (2016) *Writing the Global City: Globalisation, Postcolonialism and the Urban*. Abingdon: Routledge.

Knoch, H. (2008) Life on stage: Grand hotels as urban interzones around 1900. In M. Heßler and C. Zimmerman (eds) *Creative Urban Milieus: Historical Perspectives on Culture, Economy, and the City* (pp. 137–157). Frankfurt: Campus Verlag.

Koenker, D. (2013) *Club Red: Vacation Travel and the Soviet Dream*. Ithaca: Cornell University Press.

Kothari, U. (2015) Reworking colonial imaginaries in post-colonial tourist enclaves. *Tourist Studies* 15 (3), 248–266.

Krahulik, K.C. (2005) *Provincetown: From Pilgrim Landing to Gay Resort*. New York and London: New York University Press.

Kramer, J.J. (1978) *The Last of the Grand Hotels*. New York: Van Nostrand Reinhold Company.

Krebs, M. (2009) *Hotel Stories: Representations of Escapes and Encounters in Fiction and Film*. Trier: Wissenschaftlicher Verlag Trier.

Kulić, V. (2014) Building the non-aligned Babel: Babylon Hotel in Baghdad and mobile design in the global cold war. *ABE Journal. Architecture Beyond Europe* 6. http://abe.revues.org/924 (accessed 16 May 2017).

Lamonaca, M. and Mogul, J. (eds) (2005) *Grand Hotels of the Jazz Age: The Architecture of Schultze & Weaver*. New York: Princeton Architectural Press.

Lee, D.R. (1985) How they started: The growth of four hotel giants. *Cornell Hotel and Restaurant Administration Quarterly* 26 (1), 22–32.

Lejeune, J.-F. and Shulman, A.T. (2000) *The Making of Miami Beach: The Architecture of Lawrence Murray Dixon*. Miami Beach: Bass Museum of Art.

Levander, C.F. and Guterl, M.P. (2015) *Hotel Life: The Story of a Place Where Anything Can Happen*. Chapel Hill: University of North Carolina Press.

Linder, R. (1996) *The Reportage of Urban Culture: Robert Park and the Chicago School*. Adrian Morris, with Jeremy Gaines and Martin Chalmers (trans). Cambridge: Cambridge University Press.

Lindley, K. (1973) *Seaside Architecture*. London: Hugh Eveyln.

Liscombe, R.W. (1993) Limited nationalism or cultural imperialism?: The château style in Canada. *Architectural History* 36, 127–144.

Lisle, D. (2013) Frontline leisure: Securitizing tourism in the War on Terror. *Security Dialogue* 44 (2), 127–146.

Lisle, D. (2016) *Holidays in the Danger Zone: Entanglements of War and Tourism*. Minneapolis and London: University of Minnesota Press.

Luxenberg, S. (1985) *Roadside Empires: How the Chains Franchised America*. New York: Viking Penguin Inc.

Lyth, P. (2013) Carry on up the Nile: The tourist gaze and the British experience of Egypt, 1818–1932. In M. Farr and X. Guéga (eds) *The British Abroad Since the Eighteenth Century, Volume 1: Travellers and Tourists* (pp. 176–193). Basingstoke: Palgrave Macmillan.

MacDonald, R. (2000) Urban hotel: Evolution of a hybrid typology. *Built Environment* 26 (2), 142–151.

Mackay, T. (2017) Women at work: Innkeeping in the Highlands and Islands of Scotland. *Journal of Scottish Historical Studies* 37 (2), 155–176.

MacLaren, A.C., Young, M.E. and Lochrie, S. (2011) Enterprise in the American West: Taverns, inns and settlement development on the frontier during the 1800s. *International Journal of Contemporary Hospitality Management* 25 (2), 264–281.

Maillard, N. (ed.) (2008) *Beau-Rivage Palace: 150 Years of History*. Lausanne: Infolio.

Martin, G. (2010) *Understanding Terrorism: Challenges, Perspectives, and Issues* (3rd edn). Los Angeles: SAGE.

Matthias, B. (2004) A home away from home? The hotel as space of emancipation in early twentieth-century Austrian bourgeois literature. *German Studies Review* 27 (1), 325–340.

Matthias, B. (2006) *The Hotel as Setting in Early Twentieth-Century German and Austrian Literature: Checking In to Tell a Story*. Cambridge: Cambridge University Press; Rochester, NY: Camden House.

Mazurkiewicz, R. (1983) Gender and social consumption. *Service Industries Journal* 3 (1), 49–62.

McGinty, B. (1978) *The Palace Inns: A Connoisseur's Guide to Historic American Hotels*. Harrisburg: Stackpole Books.

McLaren, B. (2006) *Architecture and Tourism in Italian Colonial Libya: An Ambivalent Modernism*. Seattle: University of Washington Press.

McNeill, D. (2008) The hotel and the city. *Progress in Human Geography* 32 (3), 383–398.

McNeill, D. and McNamara, K. (2009) Hotels as civic landmarks, hotels as assets: The case of Sydney's Hilton. *Australian Geographer* 40 (3), 369–386.

McNeill, D. and McNamara, K. (2012) The life and death of great hotels: A building biography of Sydney's 'The Australia'. *Transactions of the Institute of British Geographers* 37 (1), 149–163.

Mentzer, M.S. (2010) Scientific management and the American hotel. *Management & Organizational History* 5 (3–4), 428–446.

Merrill, D. (2009) *Negotiating Paradise: U.S. Tourism and Empire in Twentieth-Century Latin America*. Chapel Hill: University of North Carolina Press.

Miles, B. (2001) *The Beat Hotel: Ginsberg, Burroughs, and Corso in Paris, 1958–1963*. New York: The Grove Press.

Montgomery-Massingbred, H. and Watkin, D. (1980) *The London Ritz: A Social and Architectural History*. London: Atrium Press.

Moore, J. (2014) Making Cairo modern? Innovation, urban form and the development of suburbia, c. 1880–1922. *Urban History* 41 (1), 81–104.

Morrison, K. (2016) *Sarajevo's Holiday Inn on the Frontline of Politics and War*. London: Palgrave Macmillan.

Mullen, R. and Munson, J. (2010) *'The smell of the continent': The British Discover Europe, 1814–1914*. London: Pan Books.

Müller, H. and Hoppler, A.A. (2013) Tourism in a neutral country surrounded by war. In R. Butler and W. Suntikul (eds) *Tourism and War* (pp. 106–118). London: Routledge.

Murphy, B.M. (2014) *The Highway Horror Film*. London: Palgrave.

Naguib, S.-A. (2008) Heritage in movement: Rethinking cultural borrowings in the Mediterranean. *International Journal of Heritage Studies* 14 (5), 467–480.

Nickson, D. (1997) 'Colorful stories' or historical insight? A review of the auto/biographies of Charles Forte, Conrad Hilton, JW Marriott and Kemmons Wilson. *Journal of Hospitality & Tourism Research* 21 (1), 179–192.

O'Gorman, K.D. (2009) Origins of the commercial hospitality industry: From the fanciful to factual. *International Journal of Contemporary Hospitality Management* 21 (7), 777–90.

O'Mahony, G.B. and Clark, I/D. (2013) From inns to hotels: The evolution of public houses in colonial Victoria. *International Journal of Contemporary Hospitality Management* 25 (2), 172–186.

Pack, S.D. (2006) *Tourism and Dictatorship: Europe's Peaceful Invasion of Franco's Spain*. Houndmills: Palgrave Macmillan.

Paraskevas, A. (2013) Aligning strategy to threat: A baseline anti-terrorism strategy for hotels. *International Journal of Contemporary Hospitality Management* 25 (1), 140–162.

Pasgaard, J.C.L. (2014) Tourism-dominated spaces. *Tourism and Strategic Planning* 1 (1), 35–51.

Peleggi, M. (2005) Consuming colonial nostalgia: The monumentalisation of historic hotels in urban South-East Asia. *Asia Pacific Viewpoint* 46 (3), 255–265.

Peleggi, M. (2012) The social and material life of colonial hotels: Comfort zones as contact zones in British Colombo and Singapore, ca. 1870–1930. *Journal of Social History* 46 (1), 124–153.

Penner, Ba. (2004) Doing it right: Postwar honeymoon resorts in the Pocono Mountains. In D.M. Lasansky and B. McLaren (eds) *Architecture and Tourism: Perception, Performance and Place* (pp. 207–223). Oxford and New York: Berg.

Penner, B. (2010) 'Colleges for the teaching of extravagance': New York palace hotels. *Winterthur Portfolio* 44 (2/3), 159–192.

Perry, C.R. (1999) In search of H. V. Morton: Travel writing and cultural values in the first age of British democracy. *Twentieth Century British History* 10 (4), 431–456.

Pettinger, A. (2013) The Ollofson. In M.C. Fumagalli, P. Hulme, O. Robinson and L. Wylie (eds) *Surveying the American Tropics: A Literary Geography from New York to Rio* (pp. 183–201). Liverpool: Liverpool University Press.

Pevsner, N. (1976) *A History of Building Types*. London: Thames and Hudson.

Philippou, S. (2013) Vanity modern: Happy days in the tourist playgrounds of Miami and Havana. *Architectural Research Quarterly* 17 (1), 73–88.

Pope, R. (2000) A consumer service in interwar Britain: The hotel trade, 1924–1938. *Business History Review* 74 (4), 657–682.

Pope, R. (2001) Railway companies and resort hotels between the wars. *Journal of Transport History* 22 (1), 62–73.

Pritchard, A. and Morgan, N. (2006) Hotel Babylon? Exploring hotels as liminal sites of transition and transgression. *Tourist Management* 27 (5), 762–772.

Quek, M. (2012) Globalising the hotel industry 1946–68: A multinational case study of the Intercontinental Hotel Corporation. *Business History* 54 (2), 201–226.

Raitz, K. and Jones, J.P. (1988) The city hotel as landscape artifact and community symbol. *Journal of Cultural Geography* 9 (1), 17–36.

Ravi, S. (2008) Modernity, imperialism and the pleasures of travel: The Continental Hotel in Saigon. *Asian Studies Review* 32 (4), 475–490.

Revells, T.J. (2011) *Sunshine Paradise: A History of Florida Tourism*. Gainesville: University of Florida Press.

Rhoads, W.B. (1986) Roadside colonial: Early American design for the automobile age, 1900–1940. *Winterthur Portfolio* 21 (2/3), 133–152.

Riley, M. (1984) Hotels and group identity. *Tourism Management* 5 (2), 102–109.

Ritzer, G. and Stillman, T. (2001) The modern Las Vegas casino-hotel: The paradigmatic new means of consumption. *Management* 4 (3), 83–99.

Rogerson, J.M. (2013) The changing accommodation landscape of Free State, 1936–2010: A case of tourism geography. *African Journal for Physical, Health Education, Recreation and Dance* 19 (Supplement 3), 86–104.

Rosenbaum, A.T. (2016) *Bavarian Tourism and the Modern World, 1800–1950*. Cambridge: Cambridge University Press.

Saloman, R. (2012) Arnold Bennett's hotels. *Twentieth-Century Literature* 58 (1), 1–25.

Sandoval-Strausz, A.K. (2007) *Hotel: An American History*. New Haven: Yale University Press.

Sandoval-Strausz, A.K. and Wilk, D.L. (2005) Princes and maids of the hotel city: The cultural politics of commercial hospitality in America. *Journal of Decorative and Propaganda Arts* 25, 160–185.

Sanjuan, T. (dir.) (2003) *Les grands hôtels en Asie. Modernité, dynamiques urbaines et sociabilité*. Paris, Publications de la Sorbonne.

Sanjuan, T. (2003) Le grand hotel: Le temps des 'overtures' chinoises. In T. Sanjuan (ed.) *Les grands hôtels en Asie. Modernité, dynamiques urbaines et sociabilité* (pp. 77–97). Paris, Publications de la Sorbonne.

Scham, S.A. (2013) Notes on a disappearing past: The making and unmaking of European Cairo. *Journal of Eastern Mediterranean Archaeology and Heritage Studies* 1 (4), 313–318.

Sheller, M. and Urry, J. (2006) The new mobilities paradigm. *Environment and Planning A* 38 (2), 207–226.

Shoval, N. and Cohen-Hattab, K. (2001) Urban hotel development patterns in the face of political shifts. *Annals of Tourism Research* 28 (4), 908–925.

Simmons, J. (1984) Railways, hotels, and tourism in Great Britain, 1839–1914. *Journal of Contemporary History* 19 (2), 201–222.

Smirl, L. (2016) 'Not welcome at the Holiday Inn': How a Sarajevan hotel influenced geopolitics. *Journal of Intervention and Statebuilding* 10 (1), 32–55.

Smith, D.O. (2010) Hotel design in British mandate Palestine: Modernism and the Zionist vision. *Journal of Israeli History: Politics, Society, Culture* 29 (1), 99–123.

Sterngass, J. (2003) *First Resorts: Pursuing Pleasure at Saratoga Springs, Newport, and Coney Island.* Baltimore and New York: The Johns Hopkins University Press.

Tallack, D. (2002) 'Waiting, waiting': The hotel lobby, in the modern city. In N. Leach (ed.) *The Hieroglyphics of Space: Reading and Experiencing the Modern Metropolis* (pp. 139–151). London: Routledge.

Taylor, D. and Bush, D. (1974) *The Golden Age of British Hotels.* London: Northwood Publishers, Ltd.

Tellan, E.B. (2016) Pera inns: The emergence of hosting as a business in Istanbul in the first half of the nineteenth century. *Journal of Tourism History* 8 (2), 127–146.

Thomas, G.E. and Snyder, S.N. (2005) William Price's Traymore Hotel: Modernity in the mass resort. *Journal of Decorative and Propaganda Arts* 25, 186–215.

Tolles, Jr., B.F. (2003) *Resort Hotels of the Adirondacks.* Hanover and London: University Press of New England.

Volland, J.M. and Grenville, B. (eds) (2013) *Grand Hotel: Redesigning Modern Life.* Ostfildern: Hatje Cantz Publishers, 2013.

Von Henneberg, K. (1996) Imperial uncertainties: Architectural syncretism and improvisation in Fascist colonial Libya. *Journal of Contemporary History* 31 (2), 373–395.

Walton, J.K. (1978) *The Blackpool Landlady: A Social History.* Manchester University Press.

Walton, J.K. (ed.) (2005) *Histories of Tourism: Representation, Identity and Conflict.* Clevedon: Channel View Publications.

Walton, J.K. (2012) Health, sociability, politics and culture: Spas in history, spas and history: An overview. *Journal of Tourism History* 4 (1), 1–14.

Walton, J.K. (2014) Family firm, health resort and industrial colony: The grand hotel and mineral springs at Mondariz Balneario, Spain, 1873–1932. *Business History* 56 (7), 1037–1056.

Walton, J.K. (2016) *Mineral Springs Resorts in Global Perspective: Spa Histories.* Abingdon: Routledge.

Waterton, E. and Watson, St. (2014) *The Semiotics of Heritage Tourism.* Bristol: Channel View Publications.

Watkin, D. (1984) The Grand Hotel Style. In J. d'Ormesson, D. Watkin, H. Montgomery-Massingbred, P.-J. Rémy and F. Grendel (eds) *Grand Hotel: The Golden Age of Palace Hotels. An Architectural and Social History* (pp. 13–25). New York and Paris: The Vendome Press.

Weiss, T. (2004) Tourism in America before World War II. *The Journal of Economic History* 64 (2), 289–327.

Wernick, D.A. and Von Glinow, M.A. (2012) Reflections on the evolving terrorist threat to luxury hotels: A case study on Marriott International. *Thunderbird International Business Review* 54 (5), 729–746.

Wharton, A. (1999) Economy, architecture and politics: Colonialist and Cold War hotels. *History of Political Economy* 31 (supplement), 285–300.

Wharton, A.J. (2001) *Building the Cold War: Hilton International Hotels and Modern Architecture*. Chicago: University of Chicago Press.

White, R. (2012) From the majestic to the mundane: Democracy, sophistication and history among the mineral spas of Australia. *Journal of Tourism History* 4 (1), 85–108.

Wood, R.C. (1994) Hotel culture and social control. *Annals of Tourism Research* 21 (1), 65–80.

Wood, R.C. (1992) Deviants and misfits: Hotel and catering labour and the marginal worker thesis. *International Journal of Hospitality Management* 11 (3), 179–182.

Woods, R.H. (1991) Hospitality's history: Who wrote what about when. *The Cornell Hotel and Restaurant Administration Quarterly* 32 (2), 89–95.

Wright, C. (2001) Of public houses and private lives: Female hotelkeepers as domestic entrepreneurs. *Australian Historical Studies* 32 (116), 57–75.

Xie, P.F. (2015) *Industrial Heritage Tourism*. Bristol: Channel View Publications.

Index

Aburish, Säid K., 109
accounting, hotel, 71
Adirondacks (New York State), hotels in the, 55
adultery in hotels, 38
African-Americans, hotels and, 67–68
Ali, Muhammad, 81
alienation, modern hotels and conditions of, 2, 7, 13, 49, 61
alterity, hotels and, 36
American consumer culture, exported through hotels outside the West, 77
American hotels
  consumption in, 31–32, 65, 67, 76–77
  efficiency and rationalisation in, 57, 70, 72–73, 78, 129
  and European hotels, 1, 3, 8, 13, 30–31, 57, 58–60, 66, 70
  Florida, winter resorts in, 28–29, 54
  gendered spaces in, 66–67
  grand hotels . See American hotels, palace hotels
  Henry James on, 13, 62, 63
  and industrial capitalism, 7, 20, 65
  in the post-World War II international order, 73–78
  mobile culture and, 61, 70–71
  motels, 32, 33, 34, 44, 48,
  narratives of exceptionalism and, 30–31, 58–60, 70–78
  openness of, 4
  palace hotels, 7, 8, 9, 13, 40, 50, 57, 64, 66, 67–68, 73
  permanent residents in, 35, 60–64

public sphere and, 4, 62, 71. *See also* American hotels, as public squares
  as public squares, 8, 32, 49
  relationship between home and, 61–64
  segregation. *See* segregation racial
  as social technologies, 19, 70
  technology in, 12, 31, 50, 65, 69–73, 77, 78
Amman, attacks on hotels in, 105
Anderson, Martin, 81
applied scholarship on hotels, 2, 16, 18, 44
architectonics, hotel, 50
architects. *See* names of individuals/partnerships
architectural history, and hotels, 4, 19, 44
aristocratic abode, hotels' relationship to the, 8, 16, 17, 24, 26, 34, 35, 59, 68
Armstead, Myra B. Young, 67
assassinations in hotels, 104–105
Atef, Tamer Mohamed, 118
Atlantic City, 27
auberge, as an accommodation type, 5
Australia
  Buffalo Mountains, Victoria, 9, 10
  hotels and resorts mentioned, 9, 10, 19, 28, 56, 98, 99
authoritarian states, hotels and resorts in, 21–22
autocamps, as an accommodation type, 32, 44
automobile, impact on hotels, 14, 32, 33, 54, 57, 128–129